SoLoud Audio Engine

Jari Komppa

November 19, 2018

© 2018 Jari Komppa
Kustantaja: BoD – Books on Demand, Helsinki, Suomi
Valmistaja: BoD – Books on Demand, Norderstedt, Saksa
ISBN: 978-952-80-0359-5

Contents

CHAPTER 1

Introduction

SoLoud is an easy to use, free, portable c/c++ audio engine for games.

How Easy?

The engine has been designed to make simple things easy, while not making harder things impossible. Here's a code snippet that initializes the library, loads a sample and plays it:

```
// Declare some variables
SoLoud::Soloud soloud; // Engine core
SoLoud::Wav sample;    // One sample

// Initialize SoLoud (automatic back-end selection)
soloud.init();

sample.load("pew_pew.wav"); // Load a wave file
soloud.play(sample);        // Play it
```

The primary form of use the interface is designed for is "fire and forget" audio. In many games, most of the time you don't need to modify a sound's parameters on the fly - you just find an event, like an explosion, and trigger a sound effect. SoLoud handles the rest.

If you need to alter some aspect of the sound after the fact, the "play" function returns a handle you can use. For example:

```
int handle = soloud.play(sample);          // Play the sound
soloud.setVolume(handle, 0.5f);            // Set volume; 1.0f is "normal"
soloud.setPan(handle, -0.2f);              // Set pan; -1 is left, 1 is right
soloud.setRelativePlaySpeed(handle, 0.9f); // Play a bit slower; 1.0f is normal
```

If the sound doesn't exist anymore (either it's ended or you've played so many sounds at once it's channel has been taken over by some other sound), the handle is still safe to use - it just doesn't do anything.

There's also a pure "C" version of the whole API which can even be used from non-c languages by using SoLoud as an DLL, such as Python.

How Free?

SoLoud is released under the ZLib/LibPNG license. That means, among other things, that:

- You can use it in free or commercial applications as much as you want.
- You can modify it. (But you don't need to).
- You don't need to give the changes back. (But you can).
- You don't need to release the source code. (But you can).
- You don't need to add a splash screen. (But you can).
- You don't need to mention it in your printed manual. (But you can).

Basically the only things the license forbids are suing the authors, or claiming that you made SoLoud. If you redistribute the source code, the license needs to be there. But not with the binaries.

Parts of the SoLoud package were not made by me, and those either have a similar license, or more permissive (such as Unlicense, CC0, WTFPL or Public Domain).

How Powerful?

While SoLoud's usage has been designed to be very easy, it's still packed with powerful functionality. Some of the features include:

- Multiple voices, playing different or even the same sound multiple times on top of each other.
- Adjustable play speed, volume and pan.
- Faders for all of the attributes (fade out for 2 seconds, then stop, for instance).
- Filter interface and ready filters for low/high pass, echo, etc for real-time modification of audio.
- Mixing busses for grouping of audio into different uses and adjusting their attributes in one go.
- Gapless looping.
- Queued sounds.
- Playing several ogg streams at once.
- Atomic operations for several sounds.
- "Clocked" playing for rapid sound effects.
- Sound effects synthesizer.
- Speech synthesizer.
- Support for various common formats like 8, 16, 32 bit wavs, floating point wavs, ogg, mp3.
- Up to 8 surround speaker support, easily extendable.
- 3d positional audio.
- Foreign interface support for python, ruby (and RPG maker), blitzmax, c# and more.
- Exotic formats like MONOTONE, SID and TED songs.
- Works with Emscripten.
- Virtual voices.
- Easy cleanup.

There's a Catch, Right?

SoLoud quite probably doesn't have all the features you'd find in a commercial library like FMOD or WWISE. There's no artist tools, and only limited engine integration.

It quite probably isn't as fast. As of this writing, it has limited specialized SSE optimizations. It contains no hand-written assembly.

It definitely doesn't come with the support you get from a commercial library.

While softare using SoLoud has already shipped on all current-gen consoles (as of 2018), the backends needed for those are not included with SoLoud due to SDK license issues. New backends are easy to write, however.

If you're planning to make a multi-million budgeted console game, this library is (probably) not for you. Feel free to try it though :-)

1.1 Quick Start

This quick start is for c++ developers. If you're using SoLoud with some other environment SoLoud supports, you may want to skip this and look at the chapter that covers your environment (such as Python).

Download SoLoud

First, you need to download SoLoud sources. You can find the downloads on the `http://soloud-audio.com/downloads.html` page.

Add SoLoud to your project

There's a few ways to include SoLoud to your project. Probably the easiest is to use GENie / premake4 to create the build files, and build a static library for your compiler / environment.

Note that the Windows DLL only exports the "C" API, which may not be what you want.

You can go the lazy way and just add all of the sources to your project, or you can copy the things you need to a single directory and include those.

You'll need the core files, at least one backend, and at least one audio source. For example, for wav file playing, you'll need the files from audiosource/wav.

If you go this route, you'll need to enable one or more of the back-ends via preprocessor defines. The current list is:

Preprocessor macro	Description
WITH_SDL	SDL or SDL2 via runtime dyndll linking
WITH_SDL1	SDL1 via runtime dyndll linking
WITH_SDL2	SDL2 via runtime dyndll linking
WITH_SDL_STATIC	SDL via normal static linking
WITH_SDL2	SDL or SDL2 via runtime dyndll linking
WITH_SDL2_STATIC	SDL2 via normal static linking
WITH_PORTAUDIO	Portaudio via runtime dyndll linking
WITH_OPENAL	Openal via runtime dyndll linking (high latency)
WITH_XAUDIO2	XAudio2 via normal linking
WITH_WINMM	Windows multimedia
WITH_WASAPI	WASAPI (experimental)
WITH_OSS	Linux OSS
WITH_ALSA	Linux ALSA
WITH_OPENSLES	OpenSL ES
WITH_COREAUDIO	OSX CoreAudio
WITH_VITA_HOMEBREW	Sony Vita homebrew backend
WITH_NULL	No audio device

The backend with no audio device may seem odd, but that can be used to call SoLoud's mix function manually, which can be useful in some cases such as LibRetro.

Include files

In order to use a certain feature of SoLoud, you need to include its header file. You might have, for instance:

```
#include "soloud.h"
#include "soloud_wav.h"
```

Variables

You need at least the SoLoud engine core, and one or more of the audio source variables. If you're using five different sound effect wav files, you need five SoLoud::Wav objects. You can play one object any number of times, even on top of itself.

Where to place these is up to you. Globals work, as do allocation from heap, including in a class as members, etc. Stack is probably a bad idea, but I'm not stopping you.

```
SoLoud::Soloud gSoloud; // SoLoud engine
SoLoud::Wav gWave;      // One wave file
```

Initialize SoLoud

In your application, once you have your framework up (for instance after your SDL_Init call), include a call to initialize SoLoud.

```
gSoloud.init(); // Initialize SoLoud
```

The call has a bunch of optional parameters if you'd rather pick the replay back-end and its parameters yourself; the default should work for most cases.

Set up sound sources

This step varies from one audio source to another, but basically you'll load your wave files here.

```
gWave.load("pew_pew.wav"); // Load a wave
```

Play sounds

Now you're ready to play the sounds. Place playing commands wherever you need sound to be played.

```
gSoloud.play(gWave);  // Play the wave
```

Note that you can play the same sound several times, and it doesn't cut itself off (but if that's what you want, there's an option for that too).

Take control of the sound

You can adjust various things about the sound you're playing if you take the handle.

```
int x = gSoloud.play(gWave);  // Grab the handle
gSoloud.setPan(x, -0.2f);     // Use handle to adjust panning
```

Read the soloud.h header file (or this documentation) for further things you can do.

Cleanup

After you've done, remember to clean up. If you don't, the audio thread may do stupid things while the application is shutting down.

```
gSoloud.deinit();  // Clean up!
```

Enjoy

And you're done!

Some useful notes:

Most calls to SoLoud also return some kind of return code which may help you diagnose potential problems. When loading wave files, for instance, you may want to check if the file is actually found.

Many of the calls also have additional optional parameters, and there are also alternate calls to do (almost) the same thing (Wav::load() and WavStream::loadToMem() as an example).

Finally, SoLoud has been designed so that you can ignore most of the return values. If there's an error state, such as wav file failing to load, further calls, like trying to play the wav file that didn't load, will simply do nothing.

1.2 Frequently Asked Questions

1.2.1 What does it play?

Currently, SoLoud includes support for various wav formats including 8, 16, 32 bit, float, double, pcmcia, etc., as well as Ogg Vorbis and MP3 files. Not all variants and features are supported, so you may experience some issues with strange files. As time has progressed, the libraries SoLoud uses to read these files have improved, but they are still not the reference libraries, so some strange variants may exist out there.

Additionally, SoLoud comes with a speech synthesizer based on rsynth, another primitive speech synth, a retro sound effect synthesizer Sfxr, replayer for MONOTONE PC-speaker tracker music, a replayer for C64 SID and Commodore plus/4 TED music, and a Commodore VIC emulator too.

Finally, SoLoud can use Openmpt through DLL interface, which can play 669, amf, ams, dbm, digi, dmf, dsm, far, gdm, ice, imf, it, itp, j2b, m15, mdl, med, mid, mo3, mod, mptm, mt2, mtm, okt, plm, psm, ptm, s3m, stm, ult, umx, wow and xm. (Note that Openmpt has a more restrictive license than SoLoud).

The interface for audio sources is relatively simple, so new formats and noise generators, as well as audio filters, can be made.

An example sin/saw/triangle/square generator is also available, as part of the "piano" example.

All of the above can also be fed through series of filters for additional fun.

1.2.2 What dependencies does it have?

There's no external library dependencies (apart from stdlib). However, to get audio out of your speakers, a back-end is needed. Back-ends that currently exist (but are not limited to) include SDL, windows multimedia, oss, alsa and portaudio, and SoLoud has been designed so that making new back-ends would be as painless as possible.

1.2.3 Is there a DLL / C-Interface?

Yes! This DLL can be used from non-c++ environments through the "C" interface. SoLoud comes with wrappers for Python, Ruby, c#, BlitzMax and others.

1.2.4 What's the animal in the logo?

A fennec fox. Google it. They're cute!

1.2.5 Is there a mailing list?

There's a google group, at http://groups.google.com/d/forum/soloud

---

Main development occurs on GitHub, at $https://github.com/jarikomppa/soloud$ and the issue tracker is in use.

Finally, there's #soloud on ircnet, if you want to pop by.

1.2.6 No doxygen docs?

No, instead you get documentation written by an actual human being. Granted, some function descriptions may be a bit terse or repetitive, but that's what you would have gotten from doxygen too..

1.2.7 Why not use this superior fork of libmodplug?

I'm aware there are other forks of libmodplug, which may be in better shape than the one used by SoLoud by default. However, those forks use more restrictive licenses, which (while still liberal) would require changes in SoLoud licensing. At the moment, you don't need to mention the use of SoLoud anywhere if you don't want to.

That said, nothing's stopping you from compiling a version of SoLoud that uses another fork of libmodplug.

1.2.8 Why did SoLoud move to libmodplug?

Originally SoLoud used a public domain fork of modplug, but as time went on it became increasingly clear that instead of supporting SoLoud the author would have had to support modplug. At the same time better supported forks of modplug existed, so SoLoud was divorced from the modplug code, while making it possible to use modplug if needed.

1.2.9 Can SoLoud do HRTF?

Currently, no. Pull requests are welcome =)

All joking aside, there's no simple place to plug this in currently. It's a TODO item for the future.

1.2.10 What about surround speakers?

Yes. SoLoud supports 1, 2, 4, 5.1 and 7.1 configurations.

1.2.11 Are these real questions?

Surprisingly, yes.

1.3 Directory Structure

1.3.1 Overview

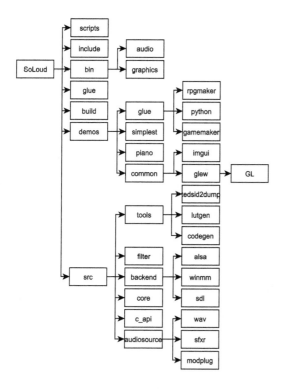

Some directories have been omitted from the overview graph to make it more manageable.

Note that documentation is not included in the SoLoud distribution, and is available separately in various formats.

Directory	Description
scripts	Scripts used to automate wrapper code generation. Unless you're adding features to SoLoud, you won't need to touch them.
include	All of the include files are kept in this single directory.
bin	Pre-built binaries of the SoLoud demos for windows.
glue	All the glue libraries for various environments, like rpgmaker, c#, python, d, ruby, etc.
build	The GENie / premake script that can be used to generate build scripts for various IDEs or a gnu makefile.
demos	SoLoud's demos showing how to use SoLoud's various features.
src	Source code for SoLoud itself

1.3.2 src

Directory	Description
src/audiosource	SoLoud's audio sources, such as speech, wav, etc.
src/backend	Back-end interfaces, such as sdl, alsa, wasapi, etc.
src/c_api	The generated c-api code, which is used to create the SoLoud DLL, can be found here.
src/core	SoLoud's core source files.
src/filter	SoLoud's filters, such as lo-fi, biquad resonant filter, etc.
src/tools	Some command-line tools under the src/tools directory. Most of these are for SoLoud development.

1.3.3 demos

Most of the demos use some common code based on Ocornut's Dear ImGui library. This is to make the source for the demo itself mostly about SoLoud and not about putting pixels on the screen, while having an easy to use UI for the demos.

Directory	Description
demos/android	Demo for Android operating system.
demos/c_test	Test for the c-api.
demos/common	Common code for graphical demos.
demos/emscripten	Scripts for compiling for web browsers with Emscripten
demos/enumerate	Enumerate all backends, show information.
demos/env	Environmental audio demo.
demos/glue	Some tiny examples for different foreign interfaces (cs, rpgmaker, etc).
demos/megademo	Compilation of many smaller demos showing off various features.
demos/null	Null driver example (using SoLoud without audio output).
demos/piano	Simple musical instrument using SoLoud.
demos/simplest	Simplest example.
demos/welcome	Slightly more complex example than simplest.

1.4 Premake / GENie

SoLoud comes with a GENie script. GENie is a fork of premake4, and the script may still be compatible with the latest premake.

If you want to build SoLoud as static library (instead of including the source files in your project) this can be handy.

GENie can be downloaded from https://github.com/bkaradzic/genie. Premake can be downloaded from http://industriousone.com/premake.

Unfortunately, GENie cannot magically figure out where your libraries may be installed, so you may have to edit the genie.lua file. The lines to edit can be found at the very beginning of the file, with the following defaults:

```
local sdl_root       = "/libraries/sdl"
local sdl2_root      = "/libraries/sdl2"
local portmidi_root  = "/libraries/portmidi"
local dxsdk_root     = "C:/Program Files (x86)/Microsoft ..."
local portaudio_root = "/libraries/portaudio"
local openal_root    = "/libraries/openal"
```

You will most likely want to edit at least the sdl2_root variable. After your edits, you can run GENie to generate makefiles or the IDE project files of your preference, such as:

```
genie vs2017
```

The current version (984) supports cmake, GNU makefiles (gmake), ninja, qbs, vs2010, vs2012, vs2013, vs2015, vs2017, xcode8, xcode9, xcode10.

You can also use one or more of the optional parameters to change the build behavior.

Option	Description
soloud-devel	Shorthand for options used while developing SoLoud
with-common-backends	Includes common backends in build
with-coreaudio	Include OS X CoreAudio backend in build
with-native-only	Only native backends (winmm/oss) in build (default)
with-openal	Include OpenAL backend in build
with-portaudio	Include PortAudio backend in build
with-portmidi	Use PortMidi to drive midi keyboard in the piano demo
with-sdl	Include SDL backend in build
with-sdl-only	Only include sdl in build
with-sdl2	Include SDL2 backend in build
with-sdl2-only	Only include sdl2 in build
with-sdl2static-only	Only include sdl2 that doesn't use dyndll in build
with-sdlstatic-only	Only include sdl that doesn't use dyndll in build
with-tools	Include (optional) tools in build
with-vita-homebrew-only	Only include PS Vita homebrew backend in build
with-wasapi	Include WASAPI backend in build
with-xaudio2	Include XAudio2 backend in build

So for example, in order to build SoLoud with sdl2static and tools on vs2013, use:

```
genie --with-sdl2static-only --with-tools vs2013
```

1.5 Legal

SoLoud, like everything else, stands on the shoulders of giants; however, care has been taken to only incorporate source code that is under liberal licenses, namely ZLib/LibPNG, CC0 or public domain, or similar, like WTFPL or Unlicense, where you don't need to include mention of the code in your documentation or splash screens or any such nonsense.

Any patches submitted to SoLoud must agree to be under compatible licenses.

1.5.1 SoLoud Proper

SoLoud proper is licensed under the ZLib/LibPNG license. The code is a clean-room implementation with no outside sources used.

```
SoLoud audio engine
Copyright (c) 2013-2018 Jari Komppa

This software is provided 'as-is', without any express or implied
warranty. In no event will the authors be held liable for any damages
arising from the use of this software.

Permission is granted to anyone to use this software for any purpose,
including commercial applications, and to alter it and redistribute it
freely, subject to the following restrictions:

   1. The origin of this software must not be misrepresented; you must not
   claim that you wrote the original software. If you use this software
   in a product, an acknowledgment in the product documentation would be
   appreciated but is not required.

   2. Altered source versions must be plainly marked as such, and must
   not be misrepresented as being the original software.

   3. This notice may not be removed or altered from any source
   distribution.
```

1.5.2 OGG Support

The OGG support in the Wav and WavStream sound sources is based on stb_vorbis by Sean Barrett, and it's in the public domain. You can find more information (and latest version) at `http://nothings.org/stb_vorbis/`

1.5.3 MP3 Support

The MP3 support in the Wav and Wavstream sound sources is based on dr_mp3.h by David Reid, and released under Unlicense. dr_mp3.h itself is based on minimp3 is released under CC0 public domain license.

1.5.4   Wav Support

Various wav file formats are loaded using dr_wav.h by David Reid, which is released under Unlicense.

1.5.5   Speech Synthesizer

The speech synth is based on rsynth by the late Nick Ing-Simmons (et al). He described the legal status as:

```
This is a text to speech system produced by
integrating various pieces of code and tables
of data, which are all (I believe) in the
public domain.
```

Since then, the rsynth source code has passed legal checks by several open source organizations, so it "should" be pretty safe.

The primary copyright claims seem to have to do with text-to-speech dictionary use, which I've removed completely.

I've done some serious refactoring, clean-up and feature removal on the source, as all I need is "a" free, simple speech synth, not a "good" speech synth. Since I've removed a bunch of stuff, this is probably safer public domain release than the original.

I'm placing my changes in public domain as well, or if that's not acceptable for you, then CC0: http://creativecommons.org/publicdomain/zero/1.0/.

The SoLoud interface files (soloud_speech.*) are under the same ZLib/LibPNG license as the other SoLoud bits.

1.5.6   Vizsn

The vizsn speech synthesizer is copyright Ville-Matias Heikkilä, released under WTFPL (in short, "do what you want to").

1.5.7   Fast Fourier Transform (FFT)

FFT calculation is based on fftreal by Laurent de Soras, under WTFPL, which lets you do whatever you want with it.

1.5.8   Sfxr

The sfxr sound effects synthesizer is by Tomas Pettersson, re-licensed under zlib/libpng license by permission.

1.5.9 RPGMaker Wrapper Generator

The RPGMaker wrapper generator contains code copied from the Ruby standard library. This is
permitted by the rule 4 of the Ruby license:

Ruby is copyrighted free software by Yukihiro Matsumoto <matz@netlab.jp>. You can redistribute it and/or modify it under either the terms of the 2-clause BSDL (see the file BSDL), or the conditions below:

1. You may make and give away verbatim copies of the source form of the software without restriction, provided that you duplicate all of the original copyright notices and associated disclaimers.

2. You may modify your copy of the software in any way, provided that you do at least ONE of the following:

    a) place your modifications in the Public Domain or otherwise make them Freely Available, such as by posting said modifications to Usenet or an equivalent medium, or by allowing the author to include your modifications in the software.

    b) use the modified software only within your corporation or organization.

    c) give non-standard binaries non-standard names, with instructions on where to get the original software distribution.

    d) make other distribution arrangements with the author.

3. You may distribute the software in object code or binary form, provided that you do at least ONE of the following:

    a) distribute the binaries and library files of the software, together with instructions (in the manual page or equivalent) on where to get the original distribution.

    b) accompany the distribution with the machine-readable source of the software.

    c) give non-standard binaries non-standard names, with instructions on where to get the original software distribution.

    d) make other distribution arrangements with the author.

4. You may modify and include the part of the software into any other software (possibly commercial). But some files in the distribution are not written by the author, so that they are not under these terms.

    For the list of those files and their copying conditions, see the file LEGAL.

5. The scripts and library files supplied as input to or produced as output from the software do not automatically fall under the copyright of the software, but belong to whomever generated them, and may be sold commercially, and may be aggregated with this software.

6. THIS SOFTWARE IS PROVIDED "AS IS" AND WITHOUT ANY EXPRESS OR IMPLIED WARRANTIES, INCLUDING, WITHOUT LIMITATION, THE IMPLIED WARRANTIES OF MERCHANTABILITY AND FITNESS FOR A PARTICULAR PURPOSE.

In any case, the RPGMaker wrapper does not claim to be Ruby or part of Ruby, and the wrapper generator and the wrapper itself is public and freely available, so that license should be covered many times over.

1.5.10 TED and SID support

The TED and SID soundchip emulation as well as tool to generate the register write dumps is based on tedplay (c) 2012 Attila Grosz, used under Unlicense:

This is free and unencumbered software released into the public domain.

Anyone is free to copy, modify, publish, use, compile, sell, or distribute this software, either in source code form or as a compiled binary, for any purpose, commercial or non-commercial, and by any means.

In jurisdictions that recognize copyright laws, the author or authors of this software dedicate any and all copyright interest in the software to the public domain. We make this dedication for the benefit of the public at large and to the detriment of our heirs and successors. We intend this dedication to be an overt act of relinquishment in perpetuity of all present and future rights to this software under copyright law.

THE SOFTWARE IS PROVIDED "AS IS", WITHOUT WARRANTY OF ANY KIND, EXPRESS OR IMPLIED, INCLUDING BUT NOT LIMITED TO THE WARRANTIES OF MERCHANTABILITY, FITNESS FOR A PARTICULAR PURPOSE AND NONINFRINGEMENT. IN NO EVENT SHALL THE AUTHORS BE LIABLE FOR ANY CLAIM, DAMAGES OR OTHER LIABILITY, WHETHER IN AN ACTION OF CONTRACT, TORT OR OTHERWISE, ARISING FROM, OUT OF OR IN CONNECTION WITH THE SOFTWARE OR THE USE OR OTHER DEALINGS IN THE SOFTWARE.

For more information, please refer to <http://unlicense.org/>

1.5.11 Vic

The VIC 6560/6561 sound chip emulator is Copyright (c) 2015 Petri Hakkinen, and released under zlib/libpng license:

This software is provided 'as-is', without any express or implied
warranty. In no event will the authors be held liable for any damages
arising from the use of this software.

Permission is granted to anyone to use this software for any purpose,
including commercial applications, and to alter it and redistribute it
freely, subject to the following restrictions:

    1. The origin of this software must not be misrepresented; you must not
claim that you wrote the original software. If you use this software
in a product, an acknowledgment in the product documentation would be
appreciated but is not required.

    2. Altered source versions must be plainly marked as such, and must not be
misrepresented as being the original software.

    3. This notice may not be removed or altered from any source
distribution.

1.5.12 Openmpt

SoLoud does not include Openmpt in itself, but can use it through a DLL. If you don't need it, you don't need to include the DLL either. If you DO need to use it, please look up its license.

CHAPTER 2

Concepts

2.1 Generic Audio Concepts

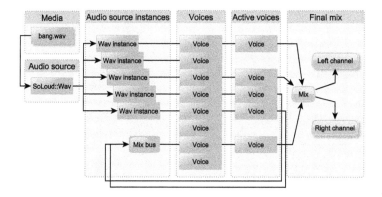

2.1.1 Audio Source and Instance

SoLoud uses two kinds of classes for the sounds. Audio sources contain all the information related to the sound in question, such as wave sample data, while audio instances contain information about an "instance" of the sound.

As an analogue, if you think of an old vinyl record, the audio source is the record, and you can put as many playheads - the instances - on the record. All of the playheads can also move at different speeds, output to a different pan position and volume, as well as different filter settings.

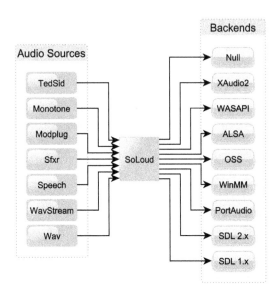

2.1.2 Back end

SoLoud itself "only" performs audio mixing, resource handling and bookkeeping. For it to be useful, it needs one or more sound source and a back end. Some other audio systems use the term 'sink' for the back-ends (as in audio source and audio sink).

Examples of back-ends would be winmm, oss, portaudio, wasapi and SDL audio. SoLoud comes with several back-ends, and is designed to make back-ends relatively easy to implement.

Different back-ends have different characteristics, such as how much latency they introduce.

2.1.3 Channel

One audio stream can contain one or more channels. Typical audio sources are either mono (containing one channel) or stereo (containing two channels), but surround sound audio sources may practically have any number of channels.

In module music (such as mod, s3m, xm, it), "channel" means one of the concurrent sounds played, regardless of speaker configuration. Confusing, yes.

2.1.4 Voice

SoLoud can play audio from several sound sources at once (or, in fact, several times from the same sound source at the same time). Each of these sound instances is a "voice". The number of concurrent voices is limited, as having unlimited voices would cause performance issues, as well as lead to unnecessary clipping.

The default number of concurrent voices - maximum number of "streams" - is 16, but this can be adjusted at runtime. The hard maximum number is 4095, but if more are required, SoLoud can be modified to support more. But seriously, if you need more than 4095 sounds at once, you're probably going to make some serious changes in any case.

If all channels are already playing and the application requests another sound to play, SoLoud finds the oldest voice and kills it. Since this may be your background music, you can protect channels from being killed by using the soloud.setProtect() call.

SoLoud also supports virtual voices, so things are a bit more complicated - basically you can have thousands of voices playing, but only the most audible ones are actually played.

2.1.5 Virtual Voices

SoLoud lets you play way more voices than will actually be played to the user. This can be useful if you, for instance, populate a 3d world with hundreds of audio sources.

SoLoud will sort the voices based on their current volume level and only mixes the most audible sounds. The number of active voices can be set at runtime. Protected voices are always played.

The maximum number of virtual voices is currently 1024, but can be increased up to a hard limit of 4095 by editing soloud.h and recompiling. Higher virtual voice counts than that will require some refactoring.

2.1.6 Voice Group

Sometimes it is important to be able to command several voices at the same time so that they are synchronized; for instance, when cross-fading between two versions of the same song.

Even if you try to unpause the two voices at the same time, it's possible, due to the multi-threaded nature of audio, that the audio engine interrupts you between these two calls and your sounds get unpaused to different audio buffers.

SoLoud's solution to this are voice groups. Voice groups can be commanded the same way as single voices, but instead of affecting just one voice, SoLoud performs the command on all of the voices in the group in one atomic operation.

2.1.7 Clipping

Audio hardware always has a limited dynamic range. If you think of a signed 16-bit variable, for instance, you can only store values from -32768 to 23767 in it; if you try to put values outside this range in, things tend to break. Same goes for audio.

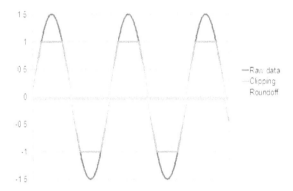

SoLoud handles all audio as floats, but performs clipping before passing the samples out, so all values are in the -1..1 range. There's two ways SoLoud can perform the clipping; the most straightforward is simply to set all values outside this range to the border value, or alternatively a roundoff calculation can be performed, which "compresses" the loud sounds. The more quiet sounds are largely unchanged, while the loud end gets less precision. The roundoff clipper is used by default.

The roundoff clipper does, however, alter the signal and thus "damages" the sound. A more proper way of doing things would be to use the basic clipper and adjust the global volume to avoid clipping. The roundoff clipper is, however, easier to use.

2.1.8 Sample

The real world has continuous signals, which would require infinite amount of storage to store (unless you can figure out some kind of complicated mathematical formula that represents the signal). So, we store discrete samples of signals instead. These samples have traditionally been 8, 16 or 24 bit, but high-end audio is tending towards floating point samples.

SoLoud also uses floating point samples internally. First and foremost, it makes everything much simpler, and second, modern computing devices (even mobile!) have become fast enough that this is not really a performance issue anymore.

Floating point samples also take more space than, for instance, 16 bit samples, but memory and storage sizes have also grown enough to make this a feasible approach. Nothing stops the audio sources from keeping data in a more "compressed" format and performing on-the-fly conversion to float, if memory requirements are a concern.

2.1.9   Sample Rate

The sample rate represents the number of samples used, per second. Typical sample rates are 8000Hz, 22050Hz, 44100Hz and 48000Hz. Higher the sample rates mean clearer sound, but also bigger files, more memory and higher processing power requirements.

Due to limitations in human hearing, 44100Hz is generally considered sufficient. Some audiophiles disagree, but then again, some audiophiles buy gold-plated USB cables.

2.1.10   Hz

Hertz, SI unit of frequency. 0.1Hz means "once per 10 seconds", 1Hz means "once per second", 10Hz means "10 times per second", and 192kHz means "192000 times per second".

2.1.11   Play Speed

In addition to a base sample rate, which represents the "normal" playing speed, SoLoud includes a "relative play speed" option. This simply changes the sample rate. However, if you replace your sounds with something that has a different "base" sample rate, using the relative play speed will retain the effect of playing the sound slower (and lower) or faster (and higher).

2.1.12   Relative Play Speed

SoLoud lets you change the relative play speed of samples. Please note that asking for a higher relative play speed is always more expensive than a lower one.

Playing samples at higher or lower sample rate than they're intended can also cause resampling issues.

2.1.13   Resampling

SoLoud has to perform resampling when mixing. In an ideal case, all of the sources and the destination sample rate are the same, and no resampling is needed, but this is often not true.

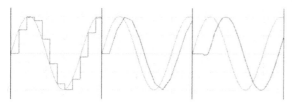

Currently, SoLoud supports "linear interpolation", which calculates linear interpolation of samples, as well as "point sample" resampling, which means it simply skips or repeats samples as needed.

Picking the resampler is done by editing the soloud.h file.

The linear interpolation resampler is used by default.

Higher quality resamplers are planned.

2.1.14 Pan

Where the sound is coming from in the stereo sound, ranging from left speaker only to right speaker only. SoLoud uses an algorithm to calculate the left/right channel volume so that the overall volume is retained across the field. You can also set the left/right volumes directly, if needed.

2.1.15 Handle

SoLoud uses throwaway handles to control sounds. The handle is an integer, and internally tracks the channel and sound id, as well as an "uniqueness" value.

If you try to use a handle after the sound it represents has stopped, the operation is quietly discarded (or if you're requesting information, some kind of generic value is returned). You can also query the validity of a handle.

2.1.16 Latency

Audio latency generally means the time it takes from triggering a sound to the sound actually coming out of the speakers. The smaller the latency, the better.

Unfortunately, there's always some latency. The primary source of latency (that a programmer can have any control over) is the size of audio buffer. Generally speaking, the smaller the buffer, the lower the latency, but at the same time, the smaller the buffer, the more likely the system hits buffer underruns (ie, the play head marches on but there's no data ready to be played) and the sound breaks down horribly.

Assuming there's no other sources of latency (and there quite likely is), with 2048 sample buffer and 44100Hz playback, the latency is around 46 milliseconds, which is tolerable in most computer game use cases. A 100ms latency is already easily noticeable. For playing drums, 40ms is too much.

2.1.17 Filter

Audio streams can also be modified on the fly for various effects. Typical uses are different environmental effects such as echoes or reverb, or low pass (bassy sound) / high pass (tinny sound) filters, but basically any kind of modification can be done; the primary limitations are processor power, imagination, and developer's skill in digital signal processing.

SoLoud lets you hook several filters to a single audio stream, as well as to the global audio output. By default, you can use up to four filters, but this can be easily changed by editing SoLoud.h file and rebuilding the library.

SoLoud also support STFT filters, where the samples are converted to frequency domain for modification and back for playback.

2.1.18 Mixing Bus

In addition to mixing audio streams together at the "global" level, SoLoud includes mixing busses which let you mix together groups of audio streams. These serve several purposes.

The most typical use would be to let the user change the volume of different kinds of audio sources - music, sound effects, speech. In this case, you would have one mixing bus for each of these audio source groups, and simply change the volume on the mixing bus, instead of hunting down every sound separately.

When using environmental effects filters, you most likely won't want the background music to get filtered; the easiest way to handle this is to apply the filters to the mixing bus that plays the sound effects. This will also save on processing power, as you don't need to apply the environmental audio filters on every sound effect separately.

It's also possible that you have some very complex audio sources, such as racing cars. In this case it makes sense to place all the audio streams that play from one car into a mixing bus, and then adjust the panning (or, eventually, 3d position) of the mixing bus.

Additional feature of the mixing busses in SoLoud is that you can request visualization data from a bus, instead of just from the global scope.

2.1.19 Queue

SoLoud also contains a special kind of audio source called Queue. This can be used to queue other audio sources. Once one stops, the next one starts playing.

This can be useful when chaining sounds, like having a never ending song by queuing random patterns.

2.2 3D Audio Concepts

SoLoud can perform 3d audio calculations. If you do not need 3d (or "positional") audio, you can skip this chapter.

In practise, all the "3d audio" does is adjust panning and play speed of your audio sources, and as such can be seamlessly used with any "2d audio" that you may also have. This means that background music, for instance, does not need to be represented in the "3d world" in any way.

Any audio source can be 3d, including mixing busses. However, true 3d positioning only really makes sense for mono audio sources.

The doppler and attenuation calculations follow the OpenAL functions.

In order to use the 3d audio, use the 3d versions of the play commands, adjust the positions and velocities of your audio sources and listener with the set3dSource...() and set3dListener...() calls, and call update3dAudio() to ask SoLoud to recalculate the proper panning (and play speed, for doppler).

```
gSndHandle_orbit = gSoloud.play3d(gSfx_orbit,
                                  50, 0, 0);
// ...
gSoloud.set3dSourceParameters(gSndHandle_orbit,
                              orbitx, 0, orbitz,
                              orbitxv, 0, orbitzv);

// ...
gSoloud.update3dAudio();
```

2.2.1 Custom Colliders

Sound sources may have a custom collider applied to them. This can be useful in many cases. For instance, if you have a river and want a water flow ambience to play when the player is near the water, you can either have a bunch of audio sources along the river (wasting a lot of voices) or you could have one audio source with a custom collider that checks if the player is near the river and adjusts volume accordingly.

Custom colliders are created by extending the AudioCollider class, which only has one function - collide. The function returns the calculated volume level. Once the custom collider class is made, you can set the collider to an audio source via set3dCollider() call. The call also takes an optional aUserData integer, which can be used to differentiate between the sounds. The same value is provided to the collide() call.

```
MyCustomCollider cc;
gSound.set3dCollider(&cc);
gSoloud.play(gSound);
```

The collide() call is made from update3dAudio() before directional panning is calculated, so it is possible to update the positions from inside your collide() function. That way you could figure out the general direction the sound should be coming from (thinking again of the river example), instead of just having a general volume fade.

2.2.2 Attenuation

Attenuation, or how audio volume decreases on distance, can be calculated in several ways. SoLoud supports three different modes (in addition to "no attenuation"): inverse distance, linear distance and exponential distance. These are calculated using the "clamped" models of OpenAL formulas.

All of the formulas take three parameters: rolloff factor, minimum and maximum distance. How these parameters affect the curves can be seen in the graphs below.

Inverse Distance

```
distance = CLAMP(distance , min_distance , max_distance)
result = min_distance / (min_distance +
         rolloff_factor * (distance - min_distance))
```

Inverse distance - Varying rolloff factors

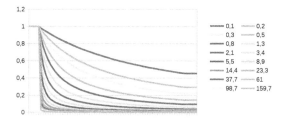

The higher the rolloff factor, the more steeply the volume drops. At low enough rolloff factor, the volume never drops near zero. Values over 1 recommended (unless you have special needs). Values less than equal to zero result in undefined behavior.

Inverse distance - varying min distance

Increasing the minimum distance pushes the start of the attenuation further. It also causes the curve to change. Note that the minimum distance must be above 0.

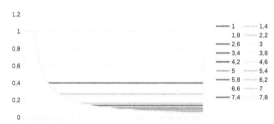

Inverse distance - Varying max distance

The maximum distance simply cuts the attenuation at the volume level it has reached at that point.

Linear Distance

```
distance = CLAMP(distance, min_distance, max_distance)
result = 1 - rolloff_factor *
         (distance - min_distance) / (max_distance - min_distance)
```

Linear distance - Varying rolloff factors

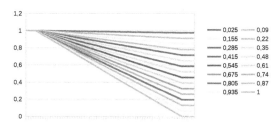

The rolloff factor for linear distance simply sets the maximum volume reduction. Using values outside the 0..1 range causes undefined behavior.

Linear distance - varying min distance

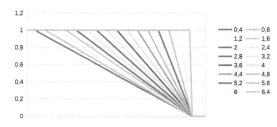

The minimum distance works as one might expect. Minimum distance must be less or equal to maximum distance.

Linear distance - Varying max distance

The maximum distance works as one might expect. Minimum distance must be less or equal to maximum distance.

Exponential Distance

```
distance = CLAMP(distance, min_distance, max_distance)
result = pow(distance / min_distance, -rolloff_factor)
```

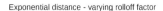

Exponential distance - varying rolloff factor

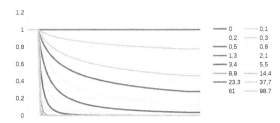

The higher the rolloff factor, the more steeply the volume drops. At low enough rolloff factor, the volume never drops near zero. Values over 1 recommended (unless you have special needs). Values less than equal to zero result in really weird behavior.

Exponential distance - varying min distance

Increasing the minimum distance pushes the start of the attenuation further. It also causes the curve to change. Note that the minimum distance must be above 0.

Exponential distance - Varying max distance

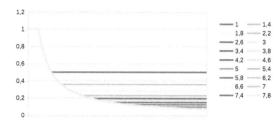

The maximum distance simply cuts the attenuation at the volume level it has reached at that point.

2.2.3 Doppler

"Doppler effect" is the physical phenomenon that causes sound sources (like an ambulance) to sound higher-pitched when they're coming towards you and lower-pitched when going away.

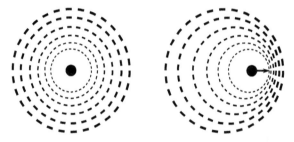

A stationary sound (with a stationary listener) receives sound waves as you'd expect. When the sound source (or listener) are moving, the sound waves get "squashed" (for higher-pitch sound) or "stretched" (for lower-pitch sound) depending on whether the sound is approaching or receding from the listener.

SoLoud uses the OpenAL 1.1 formula for doppler calculation. The calculation depends on the listeners' and sound sources' velocities being properly calculated on the application's side. If you do not wish to use the doppler, simply leave all velocities at zero.

In addition to velocities, the doppler depends on the proper value of speed of sound. The default value is set at 343, which assumes that your world coordinates are in meters (where 1 unit is 1 meter), and that the environment is dry air at around 20 degrees Celsius. If those assumptions do not match your environment, change the speed with set3dSoundSpeed().

```
soloud.set3dSoundSpeed(1497); // we're in water
```

For a bit of artistic control, you can also set the doppler factor on a per-audio source basis to increase or decrease the strength of the effect. The default value is 1.0.

2.2.4   Distance Delay

SoLoud can also delay the start of the effects by their distance. This uses the sound speed value and the distance between the listener and the sound source. Since this may be seen as a glitch as most games do not bother simulating this, it is disabled by default. To enable, use the set3dDistanceDelay() function on your sound sources.

```
snipershot.set3dDistanceDelay(1);
```

2.2.5   Speaker Output

Speakers are defined as 3d vectors, and the volume at which each speaker plays is calculated like:

```
volume = (dot(speaker_vector, sound_vector) + 1) / 2
```

In practise this ((dot+1)/2) calculation creates a field where sounds that come from the same direction as the speaker play at maximum volume, while sounds that come from exact opposite direction play at zero volume, and anything in between gets a reduced volume.

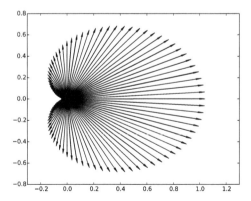

This algorithm is easily applied to any number of speakers in any positioning in 3d space. It may not be as clear-sounding as "Vector Base Amplitude Panning (VBAP)", but it's really easy to implement.

2.3 Voice Management

SoLoud supports virtual voices, meaning that you can call play() on many more voices than will be actually audible. SoLoud will then sort the voices by their set volume and play the ones that are potentially most audible.

The default behavior for the inaudible voices is to pause, and resume when audible again. This is fine for ambiance loops, for instance, but is not suitable for some sounds.

If you, for instance, have a gun that shoots every five seconds, having its output end up in the inaudible list will eat up the virtual voices, and when the sounds become audible (by the player moving near the audio source, for example), the sounds will become active at once, which is probably not the desired outcome.

```
bang.setInaudibleBehavior(false, true);
```

There are also some sounds that need to keep playing even if they should not be audible, because their timing is critical (say, a speech).

```
classof74.setInaudibleBehavior(true, false);
```

You can alter the behavior of a sound source by calling setInaudibleBehavior(), either on an audio source or through the Soloud object for live sounds. Setting both of the flags on is legal, but the sound will just get killed when inaudible.

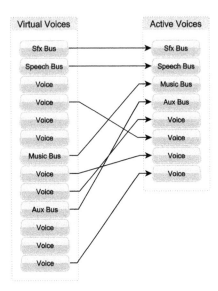

When gathering the sounds, all voices flagged as "must tick" are selected first. All busses are marked as "must tick" by default. If a lot of voices have the flag on, it may become difficult or even impossible for SoLoud to pick the loudest voices.

You can set the maximum number of active voices via SoLoud's setMaxActiveVoiceCount call:

```
soloud.setMaxActiveVoiceCount(32);
```

The higher the number, the more processing power SoLoud will require, but the more concurrent audio streams the user can hear.

To check how many voices are active, you can use the getActiveVoiceCount() function:

```
unsigned int cacophony = soloud.getActiveVoiceCount();
```

If the active voice count is constantly at your maximum active voice count, you may have a problem.

Finally, you can check the number of virtual voices in use via getVoiceCount():

```
unsigned int ghosts = soloud.getVoiceCount();
```

By default, SoLoud is configured to handle up to 1024 virtual voices. This can be upped to 4095 by editing soloud.h and rebuilding. If even more virtual voices are needed, some refactoring is required.

2.4 Examples

SoLoud package comes with a bunch of simple examples. These can be found under the 'demos' directory. Pre-built binaries for Windows can also be found in the 'bin' directory.

Along with the examples, the 'bin' directory also contains some command-line tools. These are safe to run without parameters, and will print out help when run.

2.4.1 simplest

The simplest example initializes SoLoud, and uses the speech synthesizer to play some sound. Once the sound has finished, the application cleans up and quits.

This example also uses SoLoud's cross-platform thread library to sleep while waiting for the sound to end. The source code is so short that we'll just include it here verbatim:

```
#include "soloud.h"
#include "soloud_speech.h"
#include "soloud_thread.h"

// Entry point
int main(int argc, char *argv[])
{
  // Define a couple of variables
  SoLoud::Soloud soloud; // SoLoud engine core
  SoLoud::Speech speech; // A sound source (speech, in this case)

  // Configure sound source
  speech.setText("1 2 3   1 2 3   Hello world. Welcome to So-Loud.");

  // Initialize SoLoud.
  soloud.init();

  // Play the sound source (we could do this several times if we wanted)
  soloud.play(speech);

  // Wait until sounds have finished
  while (soloud.getActiveVoiceCount() > 0)
  {
    // Still going, sleep for a bit
    SoLoud::Thread::sleep(100);
  }

  // Clean up SoLoud
  soloud.deinit();

  // All done.
  return 0;
}
```

2.4.2 welcome

Slightly more complicated console-based example, playing different kinds of sounds.

```
Welcome to Soloud!
What is your name?
>john doe
Playing music. Press a key to quit..
```

- Set up SoLoud
- Load and play looping ogg stream
- Adjust live parameters of the ogg (volume, pan, play speed)
- Ask for text input, play it through speech synthesizer
- Wait until speech is over
- Try to load and play an S3M module

2.4.3 megademo

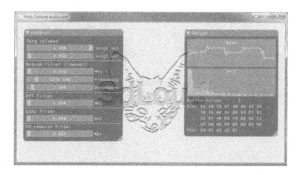

The megademo demo is a collection of smaller demos and tests showing various SoLoud features.

2.4.4 c_test

The c_test demo uses the "c" API to play voice samples as well as playing a wave that is generated on the fly.

2.4.5 env

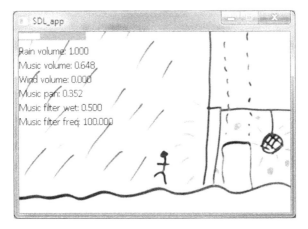

The env demo is a non-interactive demo of how SoLoud could be used to play environmental audio. It is more of a proof of concept than a good example at this point.

2.4.6 enumerate

The enumerate demo scans all included back-ends and shows data about them. Note that some backends, like WinMM, only support limited number of channels, while others may report more channels available than the hardware supports, like PortAudio.

2.4.7 emscripten

Script files are included to compile some of the demos for web use using Emscripten. These require Linux environment with Emscripten installed.

2.4.8 glue

Some simple demos are included for the glue interfaces, i.e, using SoLoud from C#, gamemaker, python, ruby, etc.

2.4.9 null

The null demo shows an example of using the null driver backend. It plays some sound and draws the waveform on the console using ascii graphics.

2.4.10 piano

This example is a simple implementation of a playable instrument. The example also includes a simple waveform generator (soloud_basicwave.cpp/h), which can produce square, saw, sine and triangle waves. If compiled to use portmidi, you can also use an external midi keyboard to drive the example.

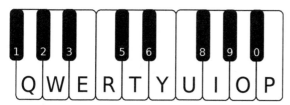

Don't worry if you don't have an external midi keyboard though, you can also jam from the PC keyboard

You can also adjust some filters and pick waveforms using the GUI. Speech synthesizer describes your option changes.

CHAPTER 3

Foreign Interfaces

SoLoud can be used from various environments through a "C" API DLL.

In order to use SoLoud from a different environment, such as Python or BlitzMax, you need the SoLoud DLL and a wrapper. The wrappers for SoLoud are not made by hand, but instead generated through Python scripts. This minimizes hassle when SoLoud gets new features, as the new wrappers can simply be generated via the scripts.

Some foreign interfaces may be more complex, such as the GameMaker:Studio, which only supports variable types double and char*. For such, we generate a glue DLL to act as translator between GameMaker:Studio and the SoLoud "C" API DLL.

All of the glue libraries, and scripts to generate them, can be found under the "glue" directory. The only exception to this rule is the C api, which is located under "src/c_api".

3.1 "C" API / DLL

In order to support non-c++ environments, SoLoud also has a "C" API.

All of the existing interfaces can be used via the "C" API, but features that require extending SoLoud are not available.

3.1.1 Using the "C" API

The glue file soloud_c.cpp can be found under the "src/c_api" directory.

You can either link to the generated DLL, which exposes the "C" API, or you can include SoLoud C++ sources (or static library) to your project along with the soloud_c.cpp file.

In your C sources, include soloud_c.h header file.

3.1.2 "C" API Example

The "C" API mirrors the c++ API.

If the c++ API functions have default parameters, two functions are generated: one without the default parameters, and one with. The one where you can change the default parameters is post-fixed Ex, such as Soloud_init and Soloud_initEx.

As an example, here's a simple example in the C++ api:

```cpp
SoLoud::Soloud soloud;
SoLoud::Speech speech;

speech.setText("Hello c++ api");

soloud.init(SoLoud::Soloud::CLIP_ROUNDOFF |
            SoLoud::Soloud::ENABLE_VISUALIZATION)

soloud.setGlobalVolume(4);
soloud.play(speech);

// ...

soloud.deinit();
```

Converted to the "C" API, this becomes:

```c
Soloud *soloud = Soloud_create();
Speech *speech = Speech_create();

Speech_setText(speech, "Hello c-api");

Soloud_initEx(soloud, SOLOUD_CLIP_ROUNDOFF | SOLOUD_ENABLE_VISUALIZATION,
              SOLOUD_AUTO, SOLOUD_AUTO, SOLOUD_AUTO);

Soloud_setGlobalVolume(soloud, 4);
Soloud_play(soloud, speech);

// ...

Soloud_deinit(soloud);

Speech_destroy(speech);
Soloud_destroy(soloud);
```

For a slightly longer example, check out the "c_test" demo.

3.2 Python API

One of the generated glue interfaces for SoLoud is the Python API.

All of the existing interfaces can be used via the Python API, but features that require extending SoLoud are not available.

3.2.1 Using the Python API

The glue file soloud.py can be found under the "glue" directory.

Include the SoLoud DLL and soloud.py in the same directory as your python files, and use

```
import soloud
```

to include SoLoud to your project.

3.2.2 Python API Example

The Python API mirrors the c++ API.

If the c++ API functions have default parameters, the same function in the python API will also have default parameters.

As an example, here's a simple example in the C++ api:

```
SoLoud::Soloud soloud;
SoLoud::Speech speech;

speech.setText("Hello c++ api");

soloud.init(SoLoud::Soloud::CLIP_ROUNDOFF |
            SoLoud::Soloud::ENABLE_VISUALIZATION)

soloud.setGlobalVolume(4);
soloud.play(speech);

// ...

soloud.deinit();
```

Converted to the Python API, this becomes:

```python
import soloud

audiolib = soloud.Soloud()
speech = soloud.Speech()

speech.set_text("Hello Python api")

audiolib.init(audiolib.CLIP_ROUNDOFF |
              audiolib.ENABLE_VISUALIZATION)

audiolib.set_global_volume(4)
audiolib.play(speech)

# ...

audiolib.deinit()
```

For cleanup, the code generator produces three functions: close, destroy and quit. All of these perform the exact same function, and it doesn't matter which you choose.

Alternatively, you can use the SoLoud objects with the "with" syntax, which also handles cleanup, for example:

```
with Soloud() as audiolib:
    audiolib.init()
    # ...
```

Here's a slightly longer example:

```
from soloud import *

with Soloud() as audiolib:
    audiolib.init()
    audiolib.set_global_volume(10)

    speech = Speech()

    flanger = FlangerFilter()
    speech.set_filter(0, flanger)

    t = "Hello Python (OOP) World!"
    speech.set_text(t)
    print(t)
    audiolib.play(speech)

    print "Enter text to speak (empty string quits)"
    while t != "":
        t = raw_input(": ")
        speech.set_text(t);
        audiolib.play(speech);

    speech.close()

print "Bye"
```

3.3 Ruby API

One of the generated glue interfaces for SoLoud is the Ruby API.

All of the existing interfaces can be used via the Ruby API, but features that require extending SoLoud are not available.

3.3.1 Using the Ruby API

The glue file soloud.rb can be found under the "glue" directory.

Include the SoLoud DLL and soloud.rb in the same directory as your ruby files, and use

```
load 'soloud.rb'
```

to include SoLoud to your project.

3.3.2 Ruby API Example

The Ruby API mirrors the c++ API.

If the c++ API functions have default parameters, the same function in the ruby API will also have default parameters.

As an example, here's a simple example in the C++ api:

```
SoLoud::Soloud soloud;
SoLoud::Speech speech;

speech.setText("Hello c++ api");

soloud.init(SoLoud::Soloud::CLIP_ROUNDOFF |
            SoLoud::Soloud::ENABLE_VISUALIZATION)

soloud.setGlobalVolume(4);
soloud.play(speech);

// ...

soloud.deinit();
```

Converted to the Ruby API, this becomes:

```
load 'soloud.rb'

soloud=Soloud.new("")
speech=Speech.new("")

speech.set_text("Hello Ruby api")

soloud.init(soloud::CLIP_ROUNDOFF |
            soloud::ENABLE_VISUALIZATION)

soloud.set_global_volume(4)
soloud.play(speech)

# ...

soloud.deinit()
speech.destroy()
soloud.destroy()
```

3.4 RPG Maker API

One of the generated glue interfaces for SoLoud is the RPG Maker API. Since RPG Maker uses Ruby, this API is equal to the Ruby API.

All of the existing interfaces can be used via the Ruby API, but features that require extending SoLoud are not available.

3.4.1 Using the RPG Maker API

The glue file rpgmaker_soloud.rb can be found under the "glue" directory.

Copy the contents of rpgmaker_soloud.rb into one RPG Maker script tab, drop the "soloud_x86.dll" in your project's System folder and just use it.

3.4.2 RPG Maker API Example

The RPG Maker Ruby API mirrors the c++ API.

If the c++ API functions have default parameters, the same function in the ruby API will also have default parameters.

As an example, here's a simple example in the C++ api:

```cpp
SoLoud::Soloud soloud;
SoLoud::Speech speech;

speech.setText("Hello c++ api");

soloud.init(SoLoud::Soloud::CLIP_ROUNDOFF |
            SoLoud::Soloud::ENABLE_VISUALIZATION)

soloud.setGlobalVolume(4);
soloud.play(speech);

// ...

soloud.deinit();
```

Converted to the RPG Maker API, this becomes:

```ruby
soloud=SoLoud::Soloud.new
speech=SoLoud::Speech.new

speech.set_text("Hello Ruby api")

soloud.init(SoLoud::Soloud::CLIP_ROUNDOFF |
            SoLoud::Soloud::ENABLE_VISUALIZATION)

soloud.set_global_volume(4)
soloud.play(speech)

# ...

soloud.deinit()
speech.destroy()
soloud.destroy()
```

3.5 BlitzMax API

Using the BlitzMax wrapper, SoLoud DLL can be used from BlitzMax.

All of the existing interfaces can be used via the BlitzMax API, but features that require extending SoLoud are not available.

3.5.1 Using the BlitzMax API

The glue file soloud.bmx can be found under the "glue" directory.

To use SoLoud with BlitzMax, you can use the soloud.bmx from the glue directory. Be sure to have soloud_x86.dll in your project directory.

3.5.2 BlitzMax API Example

The BlitzMax API mirrors the c++ API.

If the c++ API functions have default parameters, two functions are generated: one without the default parameters, and one with. The one where you can change the default parameters is post-fixed Ex, such as Soloud_init and Soloud_initEx.

As an example, here's a simple example in the C++ api:

```
SoLoud::Soloud soloud;
SoLoud::Speech speech;

speech.setText("Hello c++ api");

soloud.init(SoLoud::Soloud::CLIP_ROUNDOFF |
            SoLoud::Soloud::ENABLE_VISUALIZATION)

soloud.setGlobalVolume(4);
soloud.play(speech);

// ...

soloud.deinit();
```

Converted to the BlitzMax API, this becomes:

```
SuperStrict

Import "soloud.bmx"

Local soloud:Byte Ptr = Soloud_create ()
Local speech:Byte Ptr = Speech_create ()

Speech_setText speech, "hello from blits max".ToCString ()

Soloud_initEx soloud, SOLOUD_CLIP_ROUNDOFF | SOLOUD_ENABLE_VISUALIZATION,
              SOLOUD_AUTO, SOLOUD_AUTO, SOLOUD_AUTO

Soloud_setGlobalVolume soloud, 4
Soloud_play soloud, speech

' ...

Soloud_deinit soloud

Speech_destroy speech
Soloud_destroy soloud
```

3.6 GameMaker: Studio API

Using the GameMaker: Studio extension, SoLoud can be used from GameMaker: Studio.

Most of the existing interfaces can be used via the GameMaker: Studio API. Features that require extending SoLoud are not available. Additionally, the GameMaker: Studio limits extensions to only two variable types: doubles and strings. This means that anything more complex, such as wave and FFT data, cannot be used.

3.6.1 Using the GameMaker: Studio API

The extension soloud.gmez can be found under the "glue" directory.

To use SoLoud with GameMaker: Studio, you can import the soloud.gmez extension to your project. As of this writing, only windows target is supported.

3.6.2 GameMaker: Studio API Example

The GameMaker: Studio API mirrors the c++ API.

If the c++ API functions have default parameters, two functions are generated: one without the default parameters, and one with. The one where you can change the default parameters is post-fixed Ex, such as Soloud_init and Soloud_initEx.

As an example, here's a simple example in the C++ api:

```
SoLoud::Soloud soloud;
SoLoud::Speech speech;

speech.setText("Hello c++ api");

soloud.init(SoLoud::Soloud::CLIP_ROUNDOFF |
            SoLoud::Soloud::ENABLE_VISUALIZATION)

soloud.setGlobalVolume(4);
soloud.play(speech);

// ...

soloud.deinit();
```

Converted to the GameMaker: Studio API, this becomes:

```
soloud = Soloud_create();
speech = Speech_create();

Speech_setText(speech, "Hello from GameMaker: Studio");

Soloud_initEx(soloud, SOLOUD_CLIP_ROUNDOFF + SOLOUD_ENABLE_VISUALIZATION,
              SOLOUD_AUTO, SOLOUD_AUTO, SOLOUD_AUTO);

Soloud_setGlobalVolume(soloud, 4);
Soloud_play(soloud, speech);

// ...

Soloud_deinit(soloud);

Speech_destroy(speech);
Soloud_destroy(soloud);
```

3.7 C sharp (C#) API

One of the generated glue interfaces for SoLoud is the C sharp API (C#).

All of the existing interfaces can be used via the C sharp API, but features that require extending SoLoud are not available.

3.7.1 Using the C sharp API

The glue file soloud.cs can be found under the "glue" directory.

Include the soloud.cs from the glue directory in your project, and make sure the SoLoud DLL is in the same directory as your executable files.

3.7.2 C sharp API Example

The C sharp API mirrors the c++ API.

If the c++ API functions have default parameters, the same function in the C sharp API will also have default parameters.

As an example, here's a simple example in the C++ api:

```
SoLoud::Soloud soloud;
SoLoud::Speech speech;

speech.setText("Hello c++ api");

soloud.init(SoLoud::Soloud::CLIP_ROUNDOFF |
            SoLoud::Soloud::ENABLE_VISUALIZATION);

soloud.setGlobalVolume(4);
soloud.play(speech);

// ...

soloud.deinit();
```

Converted to the C sharp API, this becomes:

```
SoLoud.Soloud soloud = new SoLoud.Soloud();
SoLoud.Speech speech = new SoLoud.Speech();

speech.setText("Hello c sharp api");

soloud.init(SoLoud.Soloud.CLIP_ROUNDOFF |
            SoLoud.Soloud.ENABLE_VISUALIZATION);

soloud.setGlobalVolume(4);
soloud.play(speech);

// ...

soloud.deinit();
```

3.8 D API

One of the generated glue interfaces for SoLoud is the D API.

All of the existing interfaces can be used via the D API, but features that require extending SoLoud are not available.

3.8.1 Using the D API

The glue file soloud.d can be found under the "glue" directory.

Include the soloud.d from the glue directory in your project, and make sure the SoLoud DLL is in the same directory as your executable files. You'll also want to link your executable against the generated soloud_dll_x86.lib.

3.8.2 D API Example

The D API mirrors the c++ API.

If the c++ API functions have default parameters, the same function in the D API will also have default parameters.

As an example, here's a simple example in the C++ api:

```
SoLoud::Soloud soloud;
SoLoud::Speech speech;

speech.setText("Hello c++ api");

soloud.init(SoLoud::Soloud::CLIP_ROUNDOFF |
            SoLoud::Soloud::ENABLE_VISUALIZATION);

soloud.setGlobalVolume(4);
soloud.play(speech);

// ...

soloud.deinit();
```

Converted to the D API, this becomes:

```
Soloud soloud = Soloud.create();
Speech speech = Speech.create();

speech.setText("Hello D api");

soloud.init(Soloud.CLIP_ROUNDOFF |
            Soloud.ENABLE_VISUALIZATION);

soloud.setGlobalVolume(4);
soloud.play(speech);

// ...

soloud.deinit();
```

3.9 Codegen

In order for SoLoud to be usable from other languages than C++, glue code needs to be written. Most environments are able to use "C" DLL:s, and this is one of the things SoLoud has.

For most cases, you won't need to care about the codegen. Here's some information, however, if should you be curious.

Writing and maintaining glue code by hand is, however, tedious and prone to errors, so all of the glue code for SoLoud is generated with scripts.

The "C" API is automatically generated from the c++ sources via the codegen tool that is part of the SoLoud sources. In most cases you won't need to use the codegen yourself.

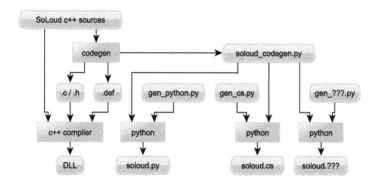

The codegen tool parses the SoLoud headers and generates the needed headers and wrapper cpp code, as well as the DLL .def file, and a Python file which can be used to generate glue libraries for other environments (such as Python itself).

The generated Python file has also turned out to be useful in writing of this documentation, as it was pretty easy to write a script that checks whether a function has been documented or not.

CHAPTER 4

SoLoud::Soloud

In order to use SoLoud, you have to create a SoLoud::Soloud object. The object must be cleaned up or destroyed before your back-end is shut down; the safest way to do this is to call soloud.deinit() manually before terminating.

The object may be global, member variable, or even a local variable, it can be allocated from the heap or the stack, as long as the above demand is met. If the back-end gets destroyed before the back-end clean-up call is made, the result is undefined. As in, bad. Most likely, a crash. Blue screens in Windows are not out of the question.

```
SoLoud::Soloud *soloud = new SoLoud::Soloud; // object created
soloud->init();                 // back-end initialization
...
soloud->deinit();               // clean-up
delete soloud;                  // this cleans up too
```

Seriously: remember to call the cleanup function. The SoLoud object destructor also calls the cleanup function, but if you perform your application's tear-down in an unpredictable order (such as having the SoLoud object be a global variable), the back-end may end up trying to use resources that are no longer available. So, it's best to call the cleanup function manually.

4.1 Basics

4.1.1 Soloud.init()

Initializes the SoLoud object. The function has several optional parameters you can use to adjust SoLoud's behavior. The default values should work for most cases.

```
result init(unsigned int aFlags = Soloud::CLIP_ROUNDOFF,
            unsigned int aBackend = Soloud::AUTO,
            unsigned int aSamplerate = Soloud::AUTO,
            unsigned int aBufferSize = Soloud::AUTO);
```

By default SoLoud is initializes with the roundoff clipping enabled, and the rest of the parameters set to auto. SoLoud will then pick the backend it prefers, and its default parameters.

Currently, you can select from these flags:

Flag	Description
CLIP_ROUNDOFF	Use roundoff clipper. Without this flag the clipper defaults to "hard" clipping to -1/+1
ENABLE_VISUALIZATION	Enable gathering of visualization data. Can be changed at runtime with setVisualizationEnable()
LEFT_HANDED_3D	Use left-handed (Direct3D) 3d coordinates. Default is right-handed (OpenGL) coordinates.

Current set of back-ends is:

Backend	Description
AUTO	Select backend automatically
SDL1	SDL1 dynamic or static linking
SDL2	SDL2 dynamic or static linking
PORTAUDIO	PortAudio
WINMM	Windows MultiMedia
XAUDIO2	XAudio2
WASAPI	Windows Audio Session API
ALSA	Advanced Linux Sound Architecture
OSS	Open Sound System
OPENAL	OpenAL (high latency)
COREAUDIO	OSX CoreAudio
OPENSLES	OpenSL ES
VITA_HOMEBREW	Vita console homebrew SDK
NULLDRIVER	Null driver

4.1.2 Soloud.deinit()

Shut down the SoLoud object.

```
void deinit();
```

Should be called before shutting down. While the shutdown probably will work out fine without calling this function, it is recommended that applications call the deinit function explicitly.

If the cleanup is left for the executable teardown, it is possible that the backend gets shut down first, and then SoLoud's audio thread may try to call it afterwards, leading to undefined behavior.

4.1.3 Soloud.play()

The play function can be used to start playing a sound source. The function has more than one parameter, with typical default values set to most of them.

```
int play(AudioSource &aSound,
         float aVolume = 1.0f,  // Full volume
         float aPan = 0.0f,     // Centered
         int aPaused = 0,       // Not paused
         int aBus = 0);         // Primary bus
```

Unless you know what you're doing, leave the aBus parameter to zero.

The play function returns a channel handle which can be used to adjust the parameters of the sound while it's playing. The most common parameters can be set with the play function parameters, but for more complex processing you may want to start the sound paused, adjust the parameters, and then un-pause it.

```
int h = soloud.play(sound, 1, 0, 1);    // start paused
soloud.setRelativePlaySpeed(h, 0.8f);   // change a parameter
soloud.setPause(h, 0);                  // unpause
```

4.1.4 Soloud.playClocked()

This is a variant of the play function that takes additional parameter, the time offset for the sound. While the vanilla play() tries to play sounds as soon as possible, the playClocked will delay the start of sounds so that rapidly launched sounds don't all get clumped to the start of the next outgoing sound buffer.

Let's say we have a short sample and we want to play it repeatedly.

If our play calls are rapid enough, several calls will hit the same audio buffer, and the effect simply amplifies the sound:

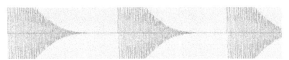

If we use playClocked instead, SoLoud will notice that several calls are being made within one audio buffer, and will delay the later ones based on the time given as a parameter, resulting in what we wanted in the first place:

The "pew pew" example gives an interactive and intuitive way of understanding how this function is used, and what problem it solves.

```
t = time_from_game_engine();            // Game physics time
int h = soloud.playClocked(t, pew);     // Shoot!
```

Apart from the delayed start, the playClocked() works exactly like the play() function, except that there's no way to start them in a paused state.

The time parameter should be your game's "physics time", in seconds. SoLoud will then use that time (as well as the time you previously used) to calculate the delay between two sound effects. If a output sound buffer threshold is passed between the two sounds, SoLoud will adjust the delay accordingly.

4.1.5 Soloud.playBackground()

The playBackground() function can be used to play sounds without panning, primarily meant for background music.

```
handle playBackground(AudioSource &aSound,
                      float aVolume = -1.0f,
                      bool aPaused = 0,
                      unsigned int aBus = 0);
```

It's a convenience function, and is equivalent to play() followed by setPanAbsolute() to set left and right channels to full volme.

```
gSoloud.playBackground(gDramaticScore);
```

4.1.6 Soloud.seek()

You can seek to a specific time in the sound with the seek function. Note that the seek operation may be rather heavy, and some audio sources will not support seeking backwards at all.

```
int h = soloud.play(sound, 1, 0, 1); // start paused
soloud.seek(h, 3.8f);                 // seek to 3.8 seconds
soloud.setPause(h, 0);                // unpause
```

4.1.7 Soloud.stop()

The stop function can be used to stop a sound.

```
soloud.stop(h); // Silence!
```

4.1.8 Soloud.stopAll()

The stop function can be used to stop all sounds. Note that this will also stop the protected sounds.

```
soloud.stopAll(); // Total silence!
```

4.1.9   Soloud.stopAudioSource()

The stop function can be used to stop all sounds that were started through a certain sound source. Will also stop protected sounds.

```
soloud.stopAudioSource(duck);  // silence all the ducks
```

4.1.10   Soloud.setGlobalVolume(), Soloud.getGlobalVolume()

These functions can be used to get and set the global volume. The volume is applied before clipping. Lowering the global volume is one way to combat clipping artifacts.

```
float v = soloud.getGlobalVolume();  // get the current global volume
soloud.setGlobalVolume(v * 0.5f);    // halve it
```

Note that the volume is not limited to 0..1 range. Negative values may result in strange behavior, while huge values will likely cause distortion.

4.1.11   Soloud.setPostClipScaler(), Soloud.getPostClipScaler()

These functions can be used to get and set the post-clip scaler. The scaler is applied after clipping. Sometimes lowering the post-clip result sound volume may be beneficial. For instance, recording video with some video capture software results in distorted sound if the volume is too high.

```
float v = soloud.getPostClipScaler();  // get the current post-clip scaler
soloud.setPostClipScaler(v * 0.5f);    // halve it
```

Note that the scale is not limited to 0..1 range. Negative values may result in strange behavior, while huge values will likely cause distortion.

4.2 Attributes

4.2.1 Soloud.getVolume(), Soloud.setVolume()

These functions can be used to get and set a sound's current volume setting.

```
float v = soloud.getVolume(h); // Get current volume
soloud.setVolume(h, v * 2);    // Double it
```

Note that the volume is the "volume setting", and the actual volume will depend on the sound source. Namely, a whisper will most likely be more quiet than a scream, even if both are played at the same volume setting.

If an invalid handle is given to getVolume, it will return 0.

4.2.2 Soloud.getOverallVolume()

For 3d sounds, returns the current volume based on the audio sources' set volume and the calculated 3d volume.

```
float v = soloud.getOverallVolume(foghorn);
if (v < 0.1) foghornTooFarToHear();
```

4.2.3 Soloud.getPan(), Soloud.setPan()

These functions can be used to get and set a sound's current pan setting.

```
float v = soloud.getPan(h); // Get current pan
soloud.setPan(h, v - 0.1);  // Little bit to the left
```

The range of the pan values is -1 to 1, where -1 is left, 0 is middle and and 1 is right. Setting value outside this range may cause undefined behavior.

SoLoud calculates the left/right volumes from the pan to keep a constant volume; to set the volumes directly, use setPanAbsolute.

If an invalid handle is given to getPan, it will return 0.

4.2.4   Soloud.setPanAbsolute()

These function can be used to set the left/right volumes directly.

```
soloud.setPanAbsolute(h, 1, 1); // full blast
```

Note that this does not affect the value returned by getPan.

If an invalid handle is given to getPan, it will return 0.

4.2.5   Soloud.getSamplerate(), Soloud.setSamplerate()

These functions can be used to get and set a sound's base sample rate.

```
float v = soloud.getSamplerate(h); // Get the base sample rate
soloud.setSamplerate(h, v * 2);    // Double it
```

Setting the value to 0 will cause undefined behavior, likely a crash.

To adjust the play speed, while leaving the base sample rate alone, use setRelativePlaySpeed instead.

If an invalid handle is given to getSamplerate, it will return 0.

4.2.6   Soloud.getRelativePlaySpeed(), Soloud.setRelativePlaySpeed()

These functions can be used to get and set a sound's relative play speed.

```
float v = soloud.getRelativePlaySpeed(h); // Get relative play speed
soloud.setRelativePlaySpeed(h, v * 0.5f); // Halve it
```

Setting the value to 0 will cause undefined behavior, likely a crash.

Change the relative play speed of a sample. This changes the effective sample rate while leaving the base sample rate alone.

Note that playing a sound at a higher sample rate will require SoLoud to request more samples from the sound source, which will require more memory and more processing power. Playing at a slower sample rate is cheaper.

If an invalid handle is given to getRelativePlaySpeed, it will return 1.

4.2.7 Soloud.getProtectVoice(), Soloud.setProtectVoice()

These functions can be used to get and set a sound's protection state.

```
int v = soloud.getProtectVoice(h);    // Get the protection state
if (v) soloud.setProtectVoice(h, 0); // Disable if protected
```

Normally, if you try to play more sounds than there are voices, SoLoud will kill off the oldest playing sound to make room. This will most likely be your background music. This can be worked around by protecting the sound.

If all voices are protected, the result will be undefined.

If an invalid handle is given to getProtectChannel, it will return 0.

4.2.8 Soloud.getPause(), Soloud.setPause()

The setPause function can be used to pause, or unpause, a sound.

```
if (soloud.getPause(h)) hum_silently();
soloud.setPause(h, 0); // resumes playback
```

Note that even if a sound is paused, its channel may be taken over. Trying to resume a sound that's no longer in a channel doesn't do anything.

If the handle is invalid, the getPause will return 0.

4.2.9 Soloud.setPauseAll()

The setPauseAll function can be used to pause, or unpause, all sounds.

```
soloud.setPauseAll(0); // resumes playback of all channels
```

Note that this function will overwrite the pause state of all channels at once. If your game uses this to pause/unpause the sound while the game is paused, do note that it will also pause/unpause any sounds that you may have paused/unpaused separately.

4.2.10 Soloud.setFilterParameter()

Sets a parameter for a live instance of a filter. The filter must support changing of live parameters; otherwise this call does nothing.

```
soloud.setFilterParameter(h, 3, FILTER::CUTOFF, 1000);
// set h's 3rd filter's "cutoff" value to 1000
```

4.2.11 Soloud.getFilterParameter()

Gets a parameter from a live instance of a filter. The filter must support changing of live parameters; otherwise this call returns zero.

```
float v = soloud.getFilterParameter(h,3,FILTER::CUTOFF);
// get h's 3rd filter's "cutoff" value
```

4.2.12 Soloud.getLooping(), Soloud.setLooping()

Get or set the looping behavior of a live sound.

```
bool l = soloud.getLooping(h);
soloud.setLooping(h, !l); // anti-loop
```

4.2.13 Soloud.setLoopPoint(), Soloud.getLoopPoint()

If looping is enabled, the loop point is, by default, the start of the stream. The loop point can be changed, and current loop point can be queried with these functions.

```
double t = soloud.getLoopPoint(h);
snd.setLoopPoint(h, t + 1); // skip 1 second more when looping
...
snd.setLoopPoint(h, 0); // loop from start
```

4.2.14 Soloud.setInaudibleBehavior()

Set the inaudible behavior of a live sound. By default, if a sound is inaudible, it's paused, and will resume when it becomes audible again. With this function you can tell SoLoud to either kill the sound if it becomes inaudible, or to keep ticking the sound even if it's inaudible.

```
// The dictator's speech must go on even if not heard
soloud.setInaudibleBehavior(h, true, false);
```

4.3 Faders

4.3.1 Overview

Faders are a convenient way of performing some common audio tasks without having to add complex code into your application.

The most common use for the faders is to fade audio in or out, adding nice touches and polish.

Let's say you're exiting a bar and entering the street.

```
soloud.fadeVolume(bar_ambience, 0, 2); // fade bar out in 2 seconds
soloud.scheduleStop(bar_ambience, 2);  // stop the bar ambience after fadeout
street_ambience = soloud.play(cars, 0);// start street ambience at 0 volume
soloud.setProtectChannel(street_ambience, 1); // protect it
soloud.fadeVolume(street_ambience, 1, 1.5f); // fade street in in 1.5
```

Or let's say you're quiting your game.

```
soloud.fadeGlobalVolume(0, 1); // Fade out global volume in 1 second
```

The faders are only evaluated once per mix function call - in other words, whenever the back end requests samples from SoLoud, which is likely to be in chunks of 20-100ms, which is smoothly enough for most uses.

The exception is volume (which includes panning), which gets interpolated on per-sample basis to avoid artifacts.

The starting value for most faders is the current value.

4.3.2 Soloud.fadeVolume()

Smoothly change a channel's volume over specified time.

```
soloud.fadeVolume(orchestra, 1, 60); // The orchestra creeps in for a minute
```

The fader is disabled if you change the channel's volume with setVolume()

4.3.3 Soloud.fadePan()

Smoothly change a channel's pan setting over specified time.

```
soloud.setPan(racecar, -1); // set start value
soloud.fadePan(racecar, 1, 0.5); // Swoosh!
```

The fader is disabled if you change the channel's panning with setPan() or setPanAbsolute()

4.3.4 Soloud.fadeRelativePlaySpeed()

Smoothly change a channel's relative play speed over specified time.

```
soloud.fadeRelativePlaySpeed(hal, 0.1, 6); // Hal's message slows down
```

The fader is disabled if you change the channel's play speed with setRelativePlaySpeed()

4.3.5 Soloud.fadeGlobalVolume()

Smoothly change the global volume over specified time.

```
soloud.fadeGlobalVolume(0, 2); // Fade everything out in 2 seconds
```

The fader is disabled if you change the global volume with setGlobalVolume()

4.3.6 Soloud.schedulePause()

After specified time, pause the channel

```
soloud.fadeVolume(jukebox, 0, 2); // Fade out the music in 2 seconds
soloud.schedulePause(jukebox, 2);    // Pause the music after 2 seconds
```

The scheduler is disabled if you set the pause state with setPause() or setPauseAll().

4.3.7   Soloud.scheduleStop()

After specified time, stop the channel

```
soloud.fadeVolume(applause, 0, 10);   // Fade out the cheers for 10 seconds
soloud.scheduleStop(applause, 10);      // Stop the sound after 10 seconds
```

There's no way (currently) to disable this scheduler.

4.3.8   Soloud.oscillateVolume()

Set fader to oscillate the volume at specified frequency.

```
soloud.oscillateVolume(murmur, 0, 0.2, 5);   // murmur comes and goes
```

The fader is disabled if you change the channel's volume with setVolume()

4.3.9   Soloud.oscillatePan()

Set fader to oscillate the panning at specified frequency.

```
soloud.oscillatePan(ambulance, -1, 1, 10);   // Round and round it goes
```

The fader is disabled if you change the channel's panning with setPan() or setPanAbsolute()

4.3.10   Soloud.oscillateRelativePlaySpeed()

Set fader to oscillate the relative play speed at specified frequency.

```
soloud.oscillateRelativePlaySpeed(vinyl, 0.9, 1.1, 3);   // Wobbly record
```

The fader is disabled if you change the channel's play speed with setRelativePlaySpeed()

4.3.11 Soloud.oscillateGlobalVolume()

Set fader to oscillate the global volume at specified frequency.

```
soloud.oscillateGlobalVolume(0.5, 1.0, 0.2); // Go crazy
```

The fader is disabled if you change the global volume with setGlobalVolume()

4.3.12 Soloud.fadeFilterParameter()

Fades a parameter on a live instance of a filter. The filter must support changing of live parameters; otherwise this call does nothing.

```
soloud.fadeFilterParameter(h,3,FILTER::CUTOFF,1000,1);
// Fades h's 3rd filter CUTOFF to 1000 in 1 second
```

4.3.13 Soloud.oscillateFilterParameter()

Oscillates a parameter on a live instance of a filter. The filter must support changing of live parameters; otherwise this call does nothing.

```
soloud.setFilterParameter(h,3,FILTER::CUTOFF,500,1000,2);
// Oscillates the h's 3rd filter's CUTOFF between 500 and 1000
```

4.4   Voice Groups

Sometimes you may want to command several voices at the exact same time. Unpausing two sounds on subsequent lines in code may work most of the time, but it not guaranteed, and in the worst case one of them will not make it to the same sound buffer as the other.

Audio buffer   Audio buffer   Audio buffer   Audio buffer   Audio buffer

← 40ms →   Audio buffer   Audio buffer   Audio buffer   Audio buffer

SoLoud's solution to this problem are voice groups. You create a voice group handle, add voice handles to it, and then use the voice group handle just like you'd use a voice handle. The voice group handles are not, however, "fire and forget" like the normal voice handles, and you have to destroy them manually. You don't have to destroy them if you keep reusing them.

Destroying voice group does not destroy the voices attached to it.

You may allocate up to 4095 voice group handles.

Example of use:

```
// Create group
SoLoud::handle gh = soloud.createVoiceGroup();

// Add voices to group
soloud.addVoiceToGroup(gh, music1);
soloud.addVoiceToGroup(gh, music2);

// unpause both musics in one atomic op
soloud.setPause(gh, 0);

// Clean up, destroy group. Leaves actual voices alone.
soloud.destroyVoiceGroup(gh);
```

4.4.1   Soloud.createVoiceGroup()

Used to create a new voice group. Returns 0 if not successful (either out of memory or out of voice groups).

```
grouphandle = soloud.createVoiceGroup();
if (grouphandle == 0) panic();
```

4.4.2 Soloud.destroyVoiceGroup()

Deallocates the voice group. Does not stop the voices attached to the voice group.

```
soloud.destroyVoiceGroup(grouphandle);
```

4.4.3 Soloud.addVoiceToGroup()

Adds voice handle to the voice group. The voice handles can still be used separate from the group.

```
soloud.addVoiceToGroup(grouphandle, music1);
soloud.addVoiceToGroup(grouphandle, music2);
soloud.setPause(grouphandle, 0); // play both musics
soloud.fadeVolume(music1, 1, 5); // fade music 1 up
soloud.fadeVolume(music2, 0, 5); // fade music 2 down
```

4.4.4 Soloud.isVoiceGroup()

Checks if the handle is a valid voice group. Does not care if the voice group is empty.

```
if (soloud.isVoiceGroup(grouphandle))
    probably_some_debug_thing();
```

4.4.5 Soloud.isVoiceGroupEmpty()

Checks whether a voice group is empty. SoLoud automatically trims the voice groups of voices that have ended, so the group may be empty even though you've added valid voice handles to it.

```
while (!soloud.isVoiceGroupEmpty(voicegroup))
{
    party_on();
}
```

4.5 Miscellaneous

4.5.1 Soloud.getStreamTime()

The getStreamTime function can be used to get the current play position, in seconds.

```
double t = soloud.getStreamTime(h); // get time
if (t == hammertime) hammer();
```

Note that time is a double instead of float because float will cause precision problems within 24 hours of playing, and eventually, in about 6 days, will cause the "time" to stop.

Also note that the granularity is likely to be rather high (possibly around 45ms), so using this as the sole clock source for animation will lead to rather low framerate (possibly around 20Hz). To fix this, either use some other clock source and only sync with the stream time occasionally, or use some kind of low-pass filter, such as..

```
mytime = (mytime * 9 + soloud.getStreamTime(h)) / 10;
```

While not perfect, that's way better than using the stream time directly.

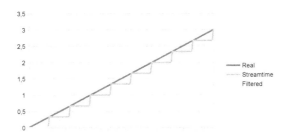

4.5.2 Soloud.getStreamPosition()

Gets the stream position of a specific voice handle.

```
if (soloud.getStreamPosition(music) > 30) past_the_good_bit();
```

4.5.3 Soloud.isValidVoiceHandle()

The isValidVoiceHandle function can be used to check if a handle is still valid.

```
if (!soloud.isValidVoiceHandle(h)) delete foobar;
```

If the handle is invalid, the isValidVoiceHandle will return 0.

4.5.4 Soloud.getActiveVoiceCount()

Returns the number of concurrent sounds that are playing at the moment.

```
if (soloud.getActiveVoiceCount() == 0) enjoy_the_silence();
```

4.5.5 Soloud.countAudioSource()

Returns the number of concurrent soudns that are playing a specific audio source.

```
if (soloud.countAudioSource(cheer) == 3) three_cheers();
```

4.5.6 Soloud.getVoiceCount()

Returns the number of voices the application has told SoLoud to play.

```
if (soloud.getVoiceCount() > 1000) lots_of_voices();
```

4.5.7 Soloud.setMaxActiveVoiceCount(), Soloud.getMaxActiveVoiceCount()

Get or set the current maximum active voice count. If voice count is higher than the maximum active voice count, SoLoud will pick the ones with the highest volume to actually play.

```
int voices = gSoloud.getMaxActiveVoiceCount();
if (fps < 60 && voices > 16)
    gSoloud.setMaxActiveVoiceCount(voices / 2);
```

4.5.8 Soloud.setGlobalFilter()

Sets, or clears, the global filter.

```
soloud.setGlobalFilter(0, &echochamber); // set first filter
```

Setting the global filter to NULL will clear the global filter. The default maximum number of global filters active is 4, but this can be changed in a global constant in soloud.h (and rebuilding SoLoud).

4.5.9 Soloud.calcFFT()

Calculates FFT of the currently playing sound (post-clipping) and returns a pointer to the result.

```
float * fft = soloud.calcFFT();
int i;
for (i = 0; i < 256; i++)
  drawline(0, i, fft[i] * 32, i);
```

The FFT data has 256 floats, from low to high frequencies.

SoLoud performs a mono mix of the audio, passes it to FFT, and then calculates the magnitude of the complex numbers for application to use. For more advanced FFT use, SoLoud code changes are needed.

The returned pointer points at a buffer that's always around, but the data is only updated when calcFFT() is called.

For the FFT to work, you also need to initialize SoLoud with the Soloud::ENABLE_VISUALIZATION flag, or by enabling visualization with the Soloud.setVisualizationEnable() call. Otherwise the source data for the FFT calculation will not be gathered.

4.5.10   Soloud.getWave()

Gets 256 samples of the currently playing sound (post-clipping) and returns a pointer to the result.

```
float * wav = soloud.getWave();
int i;
for (i = 0; i < 256; i++)
  drawline(0, i, wav[i] * 32, i);
```

The returned pointer points at a buffer that's always around, but the data is only updated when getWave() is called. The data is the same that is used to generate visualization FFT data.

For this function to work properly, you also need to initialize SoLoud with the Soloud::ENABLE_VISUALIZATION flag or by enabling visualization with the Soloud.setVisualizationEnable() call. Otherwise the source data will not be gathered, and the result is undefined (probably zero).

4.5.11   Soloud.getApproximateVolume()

Gets the approximate volume for output per output channel (i.e, per speaker). Returns zero for invalid parameters.

```
float ch1 = gSoloud.getApproximateVolume(0);
float ch2 = gSoloud.getApproximateVolume(1);
printf("Volume is %3.3f %3.3f", ch1, ch2);
```

Visualization needs to be enabled for this function to work.

4.5.12   Soloud.getVersion()

Returns the version of the SoLoud library. Same as SOLOUD_VERSION macro. Mostly useful when using the DLL, to check the DLL's library version.

```
if (soloud.getVersion() != SOLOUD_VERSION)
   panic();
```

4.5.13   Soloud.getErrorString()

Converts SoLoud's error values to printable zero-terminated ascii strings.

```
int err = mod.load("foo.mod")
printf("Mod load:%s", soloud.getErrorString(err));
```

4.5.14 Soloud.setDelaySamples()

Sets number of samples to delay before starting to play a sound. This is used internally by the playClocked() function. In the unlikely event that you may want to use it manually, it's available in the public API.

```
h = soloud.play(snd, 1, 0, 1); // start paused
soloud.setDelaySamples(h, 44100); // delay for a second
soloud.setPause(h, 0); // go
```

Calling this on a "live" voice will cause silence to be inserted at the start of the next audio buffer. Since this is rather unpredictable (as audio buffer sizes may vary), it's not recommended, even if it may be a rather funky effect..

4.5.15 Soloud.getLoopCount()

Some sound sources that support looping also keep count of the loop count. This can be useful at least to detect when some sound loops.

```
int c = soloud.getLoopCount(h);
if (c != old_c)
    printf("Looped!");
old_c = c;
```

Invalid handles and unsupported sound sources will cause the function to return 0.

4.5.16 Soloud.getInfo()

Some sound sources let you get real-time information from the active voice.

```
float reg10 = soloud.getInfo(c64song, 10);
```

If the call is not supported, or the handle is invalid, the function returns 0.

4.5.17 Soloud.getBackendId()

Get the current backend ID. This is typically the same as the Soloud::BACKENDS enumeration, but for AUTO it will be set to whatever the auto-selected backend was, or in case of SDL2 dynamic linking, it will return SDL, as those two share the same backend.

```
printf("Current backend id: %d", gSoloud.getBackendId());
```

4.5.18 Soloud.getBackendString()

Get a printable asciiz string naming the current back-end. May return NULL.

```
if (gSoloud.getBackendString())
  printf("Current backend: %s", gSoloud.getBackendString());
```

4.5.19 Soloud.getBackendChannels()

Get the number of channels the currently active backend plays.

```
printf("Current backend channels: %d", gSoloud.getBackendChannels());
```

1 for mono, 2 for stereo, various others for surround speaker setups.

4.5.20 Soloud.getBackendSamplerate()

Get the samplerate, in Hz, of the currently active backend. This may differ from the one requested.

```
printf("Current backend rate: %d", gSoloud.getBackendSamplerate());
```

4.5.21 Soloud.getBackendBufferSize()

Get the current backend's buffer size. May differ from the one requested. Some backends (such as PortAudio) may lie about this and use smaller buffer in reality.

```
printf("Current backend buffer: %d", gSoloud.getBackendBufferSize());
```

4.5.22 Soloud.setSpeakerPosition(), Soloud.getSpeakerPosition()

Get or set a speaker position in 3d space. Used to configure spakers in multi-speaker systems.

```
float x,y,z;
gSoloud.getSpeakerPosition(0, x, y, z); // get channel 0 speaker coordinates
gSoloud.setSpeakerPosition(0, 1.0f, 2.0f, 3.0f); // set channel 0 to play from (1,2,3)
```

For typical use these functions do not need to be called.

4.6   3d Audio

By default SoLoud's coordinate system is right handed (OpenGL). If you wish SoLoud to use left handed (Direct3d) coordinate system instead, initialize SoLoud with the LEFT_HANDED_3D flag.

Note that most of the 3d audio calls are not thread safe, and it is best not to call them from several threads at the same time. The good side is that the 3d audio calls won't disturb the audio thread mutex, and will thus be much more performant.

4.6.1   Soloud.update3dAudio()

Update the 3d parameters for the 3d voices. No positional effect occurs unless this function is called periodically.

```
gSoloud.set3dSourceVelocity(h, -1, 0, 0); // go west
gSoloud.update3dAudio(); // apply change to voices
```

4.6.2   Soloud.play3d()

play3d() is the 3d version of the play() call.

```
handle play3d(AudioSource &aSound,
              float aPosX,
              float aPosY,
              float aPosZ,
              float aVelX = 0.0f,
              float aVelY = 0.0f,
              float aVelZ = 0.0f,
              float aVolume = 1.0f,
              bool aPaused = 0,
              unsigned int aBus = 0);
```

Instead of panning like with the "2d" version of the call, the 3d version requires 3d position and optionally velocity vector. Like its 2d version, this one tries to launch the sound as soon as possible, which means the start of the next audio buffer.

The play3d can also add the "distance delay" to the sound, if enabled.

```
int h = gSoloud.play3d(west, -10, 0, 0);
gSoloud.set3dSourceVelocity(h, -1, 0, 0); // go west
```

4.6.3 Soloud.play3dClocked()

play3dClocked() is the 3d version of the playClocked() call.

```
handle play3d(time aSoundTime,
              AudioSource &aSound,
              float aPosX,
              float aPosY,
              float aPosZ,
              float aVelX = 0.0f,
              float aVelY = 0.0f,
              float aVelZ = 0.0f,
              float aVolume = 1.0f,
              unsigned int aBus = 0);
```

Instead of panning like with the "2d" version of the call, the 3d version requires 3d position and optionally velocity vector. Like its 2d version, this one delays the start of the sound based on the aSoundTime parameter, so that firing off sounds rapidly won't cause the sounds to "clump" together at the start of the next sound buffer.

The play3dClocked can also add the "distance delay" to the sound, if enabled.

```
// trigger boom at specific coords
gSoloud.play3dClocked(physicstime, boom, bx, by, bz);
```

4.6.4 Soloud.set3dSoundSpeed(), Soloud.get3dSoundSpeed()

You can set and get the current value of the speed of sound width the get3dSoundSpeed() and set3dSoundSpeed() functions. The speed of sound is used to calculate doppler effects in addition to the distance delay.

Since SoLoud has no knowledge of the scale of your coordinates, you may need to adjust the speed of sound for these effects to work correctly. The default value is 343, which assumes that your world coordinates are in meters (where 1 unit is 1 meter), and that the environment is dry air at around 20 degrees Celsius.

```
int speed = gSoloud.get3dSoundSpeed(); // Get the current speed of sound
gSoloud.set3dSoundSpeed(speed / 2); // Halve it
```

4.6.5 Soloud.set3dListenerParameters()

You can set the position, at-vector, up-vector and velocity parameters of the 3d audio listener with one call using the set3dListenerParameters.

```
void set3dListenerParameters(float aPosX,
                             float aPosY,
                             float aPosZ,
                             float aAtX,
                             float aAtY,
                             float aAtZ,
                             float aUpX,
                             float aUpY,
                             float aUpZ,
                             float aVelocityX,
                             float aVelocityY,
                             float aVelocityZ)
```

The changes to these parameters are only evaluated when the update3dAudio() function is called.

4.6.6 Soloud.set3dListenerPosition()

You can set the position parameter of the 3d audio listener via set3dListenerPosition()

```
void set3dListenerPosition(float aPosX,
                           float aPosY,
                           float aPosZ)
```

The changes to these parameters are only evaluated when the update3dAudio() function is called.

4.6.7 Soloud.set3dListenerAt()

You can set the "at" vector parameter of the 3d audio listener via set3dListenerAt()

```
void set3dListenerAt(float aAtX,
                     float aAtY,
                     float aAtZ)
```

The "at" vector means the direction the listener is facing. The vector does not need to be normalized.

The changes to these parameters are only evaluated when the update3dAudio() function is called.

4.6.8 Soloud.set3dListenerUp()

You can set the "up" vector parameter of the 3d audio listener via set3dListenerUp()

```
void set3dListenerUp(float aUpX,
                     float aUpY,
                     float aUpZ)
```

The "up" vector means the direction upwards from the listener. The vector does not need to be normalized. Typically this is always set to 0,1,0.

The changes to these parameters are only evaluated when the update3dAudio() function is called.

4.6.9 Soloud.set3dListenerVelocity()

You can set the listener's velocity vector parameter via set3dListenerVelocity()

```
void set3dListenerVelocity(float aVelocityX,
                           float aVelocityY,
                           float aVelocityZ)
```

The changes to these parameters are only evaluated when the update3dAudio() function is called.

4.6.10 Soloud.set3dSourceParameters()

You can set the position and velocity parameters of a live 3d audio source with one call using the set3dSourceParameters().

```
void set3dSourceParameters(handle aVoiceHandle,
                           float aPosX,
                           float aPosY,
                           float aPosZ,
                           float aVelocityX,
                           float aVelocityY,
                           float aVelocityZ)
```

The changes to these parameters are only evaluated when the update3dAudio() function is called.

4.6.11   Soloud.set3dSourcePosition()

You can set the position parameters of a live 3d audio source with the set3dSourcePosition() function.

```
void set3dSourcePosition(handle aVoiceHandle,
                         float aPosX,
                         float aPosY,
                         float aPosZ)
```

The changes to these parameters are only evaluated when the update3dAudio() function is called.

4.6.12   Soloud.set3dSourceVelocity()

You can set the velocity parameters of a live 3d audio source with the set3dSourceVelocity() function.

```
void set3dSourceVelocity(handle aVoiceHandle,
                         float aVelocityX,
                         float aVelocityY,
                         float aVelocityZ)
```

The changes to these parameters are only evaluated when the update3dAudio() function is called.

4.6.13   Soloud.set3dSourceMinMaxDistance()

You can set the minimum and maximum distance parameters of a live 3d audio source with set3dSourceMinMaxDistance().

```
void set3dSourceMinMaxDistance(handle aVoiceHandle,
                               float aMinDistance,
                               float aMaxDistance)
```

The changes to these parameters are only evaluated when the update3dAudio() function is called.

4.6.14   Soloud.set3dSourceAttenuation()

You can change the attenuation model and rolloff factor parameters of a live 3d audio source with set3dSourceAttenuation().

```
void set3dSourceAttenuation(handle aVoiceHandle,
                            unsigned int aAttenuationModel,
                            float aAttenuationRolloffFactor)
```

See AudioSource.set3dAttenuation() below for a list of attenuation models.

The changes to these parameters are only evaluated when the update3dAudio() function is called.

4.6.15   Soloud.set3dSourceDopplerFactor()

You can change the doppler factor of a live 3d audio source with set3dSourceDopplerFactor().

```
void set3dSourceDopplerFactor(handle aVoiceHandle,
                              float aDopplerFactor)
```

The changes to these parameters are only evaluated when the update3dAudio() function is called.

CHAPTER 5

SoLoud::AudioSource

All audio sources share some common functions. Some of the functionality depends on the audio source itself; it may be that some parameter does not make sense for a certain audio source, or it may be that it has not been implemented for other reasons.

For example, if you stream a live radio station, looping does not make much sense.

5.1 AudioSource class

5.1.1 AudioSource.setLooping()

This function can be used to set a sample to play on repeat, instead of just playing once.

```
amenbreak.setLooping(1); // let the beat play on
```

Note that some audio sources may not implement this behavior.

5.1.2 AudioSource.setFilter()

This function can be used to set or clear the filters that should be applied to the sounds generated via this audio source.

```
speech.setFilter(0, blackmailer); // Disguise the speech
```

Setting the filter to NULL will clear the filter. This will not affect already playing sounds. By default, up to four filters can be applied. This value can be changed through a constant in the soloud.h file.

5.1.3 AudioSource.setSingleInstance()

This function can be used to tell SoLoud that only one instance of this sound may be played at the same time.

```
menuselect.setSingleInstance(1); // Only play it once, Sam
```

5.1.4 AudioSource.set3dMinMaxDistance()

Set the minimum and maximum distances for the audio source with set3dMinMaxDistance()

```
void set3dMinMaxDistance(float aMinDistance,
                         float aMaxDistance)
```

Default values are 1 and 1000000.

See the 3d audio concepts chapter for the meaning of these parameters.

5.1.5 AudioSource.set3dAttenuation()

Set the attenuation model and rolloff factor with set3dAttenuation()

```
void set3dAttenuation(unsigned int aAttenuationModel,
                      float aAttenuationRolloffFactor)
```

The default values are NO_ATTENUATION and 1.

Constant	Model
NO_ATTENUATION	No attenuation
INVERSE_DISTANCE	Inverse distance attenuation model
LINEAR_DISTANCE	Linear distance attenuation model
EXPONENTIAL_DISTANCE	Exponential distance attenuation model

See the 3d audio concepts chapter for the meaning of the models and the rolloff parameter.

5.1.6 AudioSource.set3dDopplerFactor()

Set the doppler factor with set3dDopplerFactor().

```
void set3dDopplerFactor(float aDopplerFactor)
```

The default value is 1.

5.1.7 AudioSource.set3dProcessing()

Enable or disable 3d processing of an audio source. If play3d() or play3dClocked() are used, this call is not required, and the sounds are marked as 3d.

```
void set3dProcessing(bool aDo3dProcessing)
```

Default is disabled.

```
snd.set3dProcessing(1);
gSoloud.play(snd); // plays as 3d sound
```

It is preferable to use the play3d() calls, as that lets you set the 3d position of the sound at startup.

5.1.8 AudioSource.set3dListenerRelative()

Enable or disable listener relativity for a 3d audio source. If a sound is listener-relative, the listener's coordinates are assumed to be (0,0,0) in calculations.

```
void set3dListenerRelative(bool aListenerRelative)
```

Default is disabled. Some custom colliders will depend on this flag to be enabled.

5.1.9 AudioSource.set3dDistanceDelay()

Enable or disable the distance delay effect for a 3d audio source. Since speed of sound is way slower than speed of light, in reality we might see an explosion before we hear it.

```
void set3dDistanceDelay(bool aDistanceDelay)
```

Default is disabled, as this may be seen as a glitch since most games do not bother simulating this.

Note that this will only affect the start time of the sound.

5.1.10 AudioSource.set3dCollider()

Set or clear the custom audio collider and collider's user data for a 3d audio source.

```
void set3dCollider(AudioCollider *aCollider,
                   int aUserData)
```

SoLoud expects the collider to be there until all instances of the sound have stopped. Application is responsible for cleaning up the collider. Several sound sources may use the same collider.

5.1.11 AudioSource.set3dAttenuator()

Set a custom attenuator for the instances created from this audio source. use NULL to disable.

```
void set3dAttenuator(AudioAttenuator *aAttenuator)
```

5.1.12 AudioSource.setInaudibleBehavior()

Set the inaudible behavior of the sound. By default, if a sound is inaudible, it's paused, and will resume when it becomes audible again. With this function you can tell SoLoud to either kill the sound if it becomes inaudible, or to keep ticking the sound even if it's inaudible.

```
void setInaudibleBehavior(bool aMustTick,
                          bool aKill)
```

5.1.13 AudioSource.setVolume()

Set the default volume of the instances created from this audio source.

```
void setVolume(float aVolume)
```

5.2 Creating New Audio Sources

SoLoud is relatively easy to extend by creating new sound sources. Each sound source consists of two parts: an audio source class, and an audio instance class.

Studying the existing audio sources' source code, in addition to this chapter, will be helpful in creating new ones.

5.2.1 AudioSource class

```
class Example : public AudioSource
{
public:
  virtual AudioInstance *createInstance();
};
```

The only mandatory member of an audio source is the createInstance function.

The audio source class is meant to contain all and any data that represents the sound in general and can be reused by the instances; for instance, with wave files, the wave data is stored with the audio source, while audio instances just read the data.

Note that there's no setLooping() function - that's inherited from AudioSource, and sets the SHOULD_LOOP flag.

The audio source is also responsible for setting the mChannels and mBaseSamplerate values. These values get copied to all of the instances of this audio source.

The class should have a virtual destructor, and it should stop all the instances (by simply calling stop()). The base classes virtual destructor does so also, but due to the order the virtual destructors are called, it's possible that some data required by (still) live instances is deleted before the instances have stopped.

5.2.2 AudioSource.createInstance()

The createInstance function typically creates and returns its counterpart, the audio instance. Usually it also gives a pointer to itself to the audio instance.

5.2.3 AudioSourceInstance class

```
class ExampleInstance : public AudioSourceInstance
{
public:
  virtual void getAudio(float *aBuffer, int aSamples);
  virtual int hasEnded();
  virtual void seek(float aSeconds, float *mScratch, int mScratchSize);
  virtual int rewind();
};
```

The getAudio and hasEnded methods are mandatory. Seek and rewind are optional.

The audio instance is meant as the "play head" for a sound source. Most of the data should be in the audio source, while audio instance may contain more logic.

5.2.4 AudioSourceInstance.getAudio()

SoLoud requests samples from the sound instance using the getAudio function. If the instance generates more than one channel (i.e, stereo sound), the expected sample data first has the first channel samples, then second channel samples, etc.

So, if 1024 samples are requested from a stereo audio source, the first 1024 floats should be for the first channel, and the next 1024 samples should be for the second channel.

The getAudio function is also responsible for handling looping, if the audio source supports it. See the implementations of existing sound sources for more details.

If the audio source runs out of data, the rest of the buffer should be set to zero.

5.2.5 AudioSourceInstance.hasEnded()

After mixing, SoLoud asks all audio instances whether they have ended, and if they have, it will free the object and free the channel. Supporting looping will likely affect the implementation of this function.

5.2.6 AudioSourceInstance.seek()

Optionally, you can implement a seek function. The base implementation will simply request (and discard) samples from the sound source until the desired position has been reached; for many sound sources, a smarter way exists.

5.2.7 AudioSourceInstance.rewind()

To enable the base implementation of seek to seek backwards from the current play position, sound source may implement the rewind function. In most cases the rewind is easier to implement than actual smart seeking.

5.2.8 AudioSourceInstance.getInfo()

Optionally, you can provide the getInfo() interface to let the application query real-time information about your audio source. This information may be channel volumes, register values, or some other information of interest.

5.3 SoLoud::Wav

The SoLoud::Wav class represents a wave sound effect. The source files may be in various RIFF WAV file formats FLAC, MP3 or Ogg Vorbis files.

The sounds are loaded and converted to float samples, which means that every second of a 44100Hz stereo sound takes about 350kB of memory. The good side is, after loading, the use of these samples are very lightweight, as their processing is mostly just a memory copy.

For lengthy samples like background music, you may want to use SoLoud::WavStream instead. The Wav is all about speed, and always decodes the whole sample into memory at load time.

5.3.1 Wav.load()

The wav loader takes just one parameter, the file name:

```
void load(const char *aFilename); // File to load
```

If loading fails, the sample will be silent.

```
SoLoud::Wav boom;
boom.load("boom.wav");
```

If the loading function is called while there are instances playing, the result is undefined (most likely a crash).

5.3.2 Wav.loadMem()

Alternate way of loading samples is to read from a memory buffer.

```
result loadMem(unsigned char *aMem, int aLength,
               bool aCopy, bool aTakeOwnership);
```

If loading fails, the sample will be silent.

```
SoLoud::Wav boom;
boom.loadMem(boomMemoryResource, boomMemoryResourceLength);
```

SoLoud function assumes that the pointer and the data pointed will be valid as long as SoLoud needs them. You can use the aCopy parameter to tell SoLoud to take a copy of the data instead of using the pointers directly, and the aTakeOwnership parameter to tell SoLoud to free the pointer when the object is being destroyed.

5.3.3 Wav.loadFile()

The loadFile() can be used to load audio from a SoLoud::File object. This is useful for integrating with virtual filesystems / packfiles, such as PhysFS.

5.3.4 Wav.loadRawWave(), Wav.loadRawWave8(), Wav.loadRawWave16()

It is also possible to turn an array of raw wave data into a SoLoud Wav object using the load-RawWave family of functions. These functions differ primarily by the format of wave data they load - floats, unsigned 8 bit and signed 16 bit samples.

```
result loadRawWave8(unsigned char *aMem,
                    unsigned int aLength,
                    float aSamplerate = 44100.0f,
                    unsigned int aChannels = 1);
result loadRawWave16(short *aMem,
                     unsigned int aLength,
                     float aSamplerate = 44100.0f,
                     unsigned int aChannels = 1);
result loadRawWave(float *aMem,
                   unsigned int aLength,
                   float aSamplerate = 44100.0f,
                   unsigned int aChannels = 1,
                   bool aCopy = false,
                   bool aTakeOwnership = true);
```

The variant that loads float samples additionally lets you decice whether SoLoud should make a copy of the data (such as when the data is in stack), and whether SoLoud should take ownership of the data (i.e, should SoLoud delete the data when the object is destroyed).

5.3.5 Wav.setLooping()

This function can be used to set the wave to loop.

```
gDrumloop.setLooping(1);
```

Calling this function will not affect "live" sound sources.

5.3.6 Wav.setFilter()

As with any other audio source, you can attach filters to wave audio sources.

```
gHipster.setFilter(0, &gLofi);
```

5.3.7 Wav.stop()

You can stop all instances of a wave sound source with stop(). This is equivalent of calling soloud.stopAudioSource() with the sound source.

```
gHammertime.stop();
```

5.3.8 Wav.getLength()

The length, in seconds, of this wave can be queried with this function.

```
double t = gRecord.getLength();
```

5.3.9 Wav.setInaudibleBehavior()

Set the inaudible behavior of the sound. By default, if a sound is inaudible, it's paused, and will resume when it becomes audible again. With this function you can tell SoLoud to either kill the sound if it becomes inaudible, or to keep ticking the sound even if it's inaudible.

```
// Keep on talking even if I'm not around
gSpeech.setInaudibleBehavior(true, false);
```

5.3.10 Wav.setVolume()

Set the default volume of the instances created from this audio source.

```
gTinyVoice.setVolume(0.1);
```

5.3.11 Wav.setLoopPoint(), Wav.getLoopPoint()

If looping is enabled, the loop point is, by default, the start of the stream. The loop point can be changed, and current loop point can be queried with these functions.

```
double t = snd.getLoopPoint();
snd.setLoopPoint(t + 1); // skip 1 second more when looping
...
snd.setLoopPoint(0); // loop from start
```

5.3.12 Inherited 3d audio interfaces

Like all other audio sources, Wav inherits the 3d audio interfaces. Please refer to the 3d audio chapter for details on:

- Wav.set3dMinMaxDistance()
- Wav.set3dAttenuation()
- Wav.set3dDopplerFactor()
- Wav.set3dProcessing()
- Wav.set3dListenerRelative()
- Wav.set3dDistanceDelay()
- Wav.set3dCollider()
- Wav.set3dAttenuator()

5.4   SoLoud::WavStream

The SoLoud::WavStream class represents a wave sound effect that is streamed off disk while it's playing. The source files may be in various RIFF WAV file formats, FLAC, MP3 or Ogg Vorbis files.

The sounds are loaded in pieces while they are playing, which takes more processing power than playing samples from memory, but they require much less memory.

For short or often used samples, you may want to use SoLoud::Wav instead.

5.4.1   WavStream.load()

The wav loader takes just one parameter, the file name:

```
result load(const char *aFilename); // File to load
```

If loading fails, the function will return an error code.

```
SoLoud::WavStream muzak;
muzak.load("elevator.ogg");
```

If the loading function is called while there are instances playing, the result is undefined (most likely a crash).

5.4.2   WavStream.loadFile()

The loadFile() can be used to load audio from a SoLoud::File object. This is useful for integrating with virtual filesystems / packfiles, such as PhysFS.

5.4.3 WavStream.loadMem()

Alternate way of loading samples is to read from a memory buffer.

```
result loadMem(unsigned char *aMem, int aLength,
               bool aCopy, bool aTakeOwnership);
```

If loading fails, the sample will be silent.

```
SoLoud::WavStream boom;
boom.loadMem(boomMemoryResource, boomMemoryResourceLength);
```

SoLoud function assumes that the pointer and the data pointed will be valid as long as SoLoud needs them. You can use the aCopy parameter to tell SoLoud to take a copy of the data instead of using the pointers directly, and the aTakeOwnership parameter to tell SoLoud to free the pointer when the object is being destroyed.

5.4.4 WavStream.loadToMem()

The loadToMem() tells SoLoud to load the whole file to a memory buffer and stream it from there. This is similar as to using the Wav object, except that the data is not decoded to raw samples on load.

This can be useful if you expect the media the data resides on to be slow or busy, but don't want to spend the memory for the completely decoded audio data.

5.4.5 WavStream.loadFileToMem()

The loadFileToMem() function performs the memory loading of loadToMem() using SoLoud::File objects, same way as loadFile() does.

5.4.6 WavStream.setLooping()

This function can be used to set the wav stream to loop.

```
soundtrack.setLooping(1);
```

Calling this function will not affect "live" sound sources.

5.4.7   WavStream.setFilter()

As with any other audio source, you can attach filters to wav stream audio sources.

```
gHipster.setFilter(0, &gLofi);
```

5.4.8   WavStream.stop()

You can stop all instances of a wav stream sound source with stop(). This is equivalent of calling soloud.stopAudioSource() with the sound source.

```
gHammertime.stop();
```

5.4.9   WavStream.getLength()

The length, in seconds, of this wav stream can be queried with this function.

```
double t = gRecord.getLength();
```

5.4.10   WavStream.setInaudibleBehavior()

Set the inaudible behavior of the sound. By default, if a sound is inaudible, it's paused, and will resume when it becomes audible again. With this function you can tell SoLoud to either kill the sound if it becomes inaudible, or to keep ticking the sound even if it's inaudible.

```
// Keep on talking even if I'm not around
gSpeech.setInaudibleBehavior(true, false);
```

5.4.11   WavStream.setVolume()

Set the default volume of the instances created from this audio source.

```
gTinyVoice.setVolume(0.1);
```

5.4.12 WavStream.setLoopPoint(), WavStream.getLoopPoint()

If looping is enabled, the loop point is, by default, the start of the stream. The loop point can be changed, and current loop point can be queried with these functions.

```
double t = snd.getLoopPoint();
snd.setLoopPoint(t + 1); // skip 1 second more when looping
...
snd.setLoopPoint(0); // loop from start
```

5.4.13 Inherited 3d audio interfaces

Like all other audio sources, WavStream inherits the 3d audio interfaces. Please refer to the 3d audio chapter for details on:

- WavStream.set3dMinMaxDistance()
- WavStream.set3dAttenuation()
- WavStream.set3dDopplerFactor()
- WavStream.set3dProcessing()
- WavStream.set3dListenerRelative()
- WavStream.set3dDistanceDelay()
- WavStream.set3dCollider()
- WavStream.set3dAttenuator()

5.5 SoLoud::Speech

The SoLoud::Speech class implements a simple Klatt-style formant speech synthesizer. It's barely legible, not really human-like, but it's free, and it's here.

Adjusting the speech synthesizer's output with audio filters should allow for various voices, which, along with subtitles, will let you add voice to your games cheaply.

For more serious use, feel free to study the source code and play with the various internal parameters, as well as apply various filters to the sound.

For legal notes, please see the license page.

5.5.1 Speech.setText()

The setText function can be used to set the text to be spoken.

```
SoLoud::Speech sp;
sp.setText("Hello world.  You will be assimilated.");
```

If the setText function is called while speech is playing, SoLoud stops any playing instances to avoid crashing.

Trying to set the text to NULL will return an error code.

5.5.2 Speech.setParams()

The speech's voice can be adjusted by changing the parameters;

```
result Speech::setParams(unsigned int aBaseFrequency,
                         float aBaseSpeed,
                         float aBaseDeclination,
                         int aBaseWaveform)
```

The default parameters for these are 1330 for frequecy, 10 for speed, 0.5 for declination and KW_SQUARE as waveform. The easiest way to understand what these parameters do and how they affect the voice is to play with the "speechfilter" demo that is part of the megademo example.

5.5.3   Speech.setLooping()

This function can be used to set the speech to loop.

```
gHeyListen.setLooping(1);
```

Calling this function will not affect "live" sound sources.

5.5.4   Speech.setFilter()

As with any other audio source, you can attach filters to speech audio sources.

```
gRobot.setFilter(0, &gRobotize);
```

5.5.5   Speech.stop()

You can stop all instances of a speech sound source with stop(). This is equivalent of calling soloud.stopAudioSource() with the sound source.

```
gHeyListen.stop(); // shut up already!
```

5.5.6   Speech.setInaudibleBehavior()

Set the inaudible behavior of the sound. By default, if a sound is inaudible, it's paused, and will resume when it becomes audible again. With this function you can tell SoLoud to either kill the sound if it becomes inaudible, or to keep ticking the sound even if it's inaudible.

```
// Keep on talking even if I'm not around
gSpeech.setInaudibleBehavior(true, false);
```

5.5.7   Speech.setVolume()

Set the default volume of the instances created from this audio source.

```
gTinyVoice.setVolume(0.1);
```

5.5.8 Speech.setLoopPoint(), Speech.getLoopPoint()

If looping is enabled, the loop point is, by default, the start of the stream. The loop point can be changed, and current loop point can be queried with these functions.

```
double t = snd.getLoopPoint();
snd.setLoopPoint(t + 1); // skip 1 second more when looping
...
snd.setLoopPoint(0); // loop from start
```

5.5.9 Inherited 3d audio interfaces

Like all other audio sources, Speech inherits the 3d audio interfaces. Please refer to the 3d audio chapter for details on:

- Speech.set3dMinMaxDistance()
- Speech.set3dAttenuation()
- Speech.set3dDopplerFactor()
- Speech.set3dProcessing()
- Speech.set3dListenerRelative()
- Speech.set3dDistanceDelay()
- Speech.set3dCollider()
- Speech.set3dAttenuator()

5.6   SoLoud::Sfxr

The SoLoud::Sfxr is a "retro" sound effect synthesizer based on the original Sfxr by Tomas Pettersson.

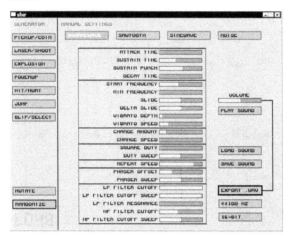

The original sfxr tool was designed to easily generate sound effects for Ludum Dare 48h games. SoLoud includes the same engine built in, so you can (should you wish) make every coin, explosion etc. sound different.

The Sfxr sound sources also include a pseudo-random number generator which should probably be moved to more general use at some point.

5.6.1   Sfxr.loadPreset()

You can simply tell Sfxr to use one of the presets (COIN, LASER, EXPLOSION, POWERUP, HURT, JUMP, BLIP). Each of the presets has several random components, so you can get virtually unlimited variations of each. (Not all variants sound good, though).

```
void loadPreset(int aPresetNo, int aRandSeed); // Preset to load
```

If loading fails, the function returns an error code.

```
SoLoud::Sfxr coin;
coin.loadPreset(Sfxr::COIN, 3247);
```

5.6.2 Sfxr.loadParams()

Effect parameters can also be loaded from a configuration file saved from the sfxr tool.

```
result loadParams(const char *aFilename); // File to load
```

If loading fails, the function returns an error code.

```
SoLoud::Sfxr boom;
boom.loadParams("boom.sfx");
```

5.6.3 Sfxr.loadParamsMem()

Alternate way of loading the parameters is to read from a memory buffer.

```
result loadParamsMem(unsigned char *aMem, int aLength,
                     bool aCopy, bool aTakeOwnership);
```

The aTakeOwnership parameter can be used to tell SoLoud to free the pointer once it's done with it. The aCopy parameter is here for compatibility with the other loadMem functions.

5.6.4 Sfxr.loadParamsFile()

The loadFile() can be used to load parameters from a SoLoud::File object. This is useful for integrating with virtual filesystems / packfiles, such as PhysFS.

5.6.5 Sfxr.resetParams()

This function resets all of the Sfxr parameters to a "sensible" default. Used by loadPreset(), which then only adjusts a few parameters over the defaults.

5.6.6 Sfxr.setLooping()

Adjusting the looping of a sfxr sound does not currently have any effect. The sounds do not loop.

5.6.7 Sfxr.setFilter()

As with any other audio source, you can attach filters to Sfxr audio sources.

```
gMusic.setFilter(0, &gLofi);
```

5.6.8 Sfxr.stop()

You can stop all instances of a Sfxr sound source with stop(). This is equivalent of calling soloud.stopAudioSource() with the sound source.

```
gBoom.stop();
```

5.6.9 Sfxr.setInaudibleBehavior()

Set the inaudible behavior of the sound. By default, if a sound is inaudible, it's paused, and will resume when it becomes audible again. With this function you can tell SoLoud to either kill the sound if it becomes inaudible, or to keep ticking the sound even if it's inaudible.

```
// Keep on talking even if I'm not around
gSpeech.setInaudibleBehavior(true, false);
```

5.6.10 Sfxr.setVolume()

Set the default volume of the instances created from this audio source.

```
gTinyVoice.setVolume(0.1);
```

5.6.11 Sfxr.setLoopPoint(), Sfxr.getLoopPoint()

If looping is enabled, the loop point is, by default, the start of the stream. The loop point can be changed, and current loop point can be queried with these functions.

```
double t = snd.getLoopPoint();
snd.setLoopPoint(t + 1); // skip 1 second more when looping
...
snd.setLoopPoint(0); // loop from start
```

5.6.12 Prg.srand()

Initializes the pseudo-random number generator to a seed number.

rnd.srand(7);

5.6.13 Prg.rand()

Returns the next 32bit pseudo-random number.

if (rnd.rand() & 1) printf("Heads"); else printf("Tails");

5.6.14 Inherited 3d audio interfaces

Like all other audio sources, Sfxr inherits the 3d audio interfaces. Please refer to the 3d audio chapter for details on:

- Sfxr.set3dMinMaxDistance()
- Sfxr.set3dAttenuation()
- Sfxr.set3dDopplerFactor()
- Sfxr.set3dProcessing()
- Sfxr.set3dListenerRelative()
- Sfxr.set3dDistanceDelay()
- Sfxr.set3dCollider()
- Sfxr.set3dAttenuator()

5.7 SoLoud::Openmpt

Openmpt is a module-playing engine, capable of replaying wide variety of multichannel music (669, amf, ams, dbm, digi, dmf, dsm, far, gdm, ice, imf, it, itp, j2b, m15, mdl, med, mid, mo3, mod, mptm, mt2, mtm, okt, plm, psm, ptm, s3m, stm, ult, umx, wow, xm). It also loads wav files, and may support wider support for wav files than the stand-alone wav audio source.

SoLoud uses Openmpt through DLL, available from https://lib.openmpt.org/. Note that Openmpt has a more restrictive license than SoLoud, so be sure to check the license.

The midi formats (.mid and .abc) require a library of instruments (patches) to be available. One free set can be downloaded from the SoLoud downloads page.

If the DLL is not available, the SoLoud::Openmpt interfaces will silently fail.

5.7.1 Openmpt.load()

You tell Openmpt to load a file with the load function:

```
result load(const char *aFilename); // File to load
```

If loading fails, the function returns an error code.

```
SoLoud::Openmpt spacedeb;
spacedeb.load("spacedeb.mod");
```

5.7.2 Openmpt.loadFile()

The loadFile() can be used to load audio from a SoLoud::File object. This is useful for integrating with virtual filesystems / packfiles, such as PhysFS.

5.7.3 Openmpt.loadMem()

Alternate way of loading the file is to read from a memory buffer.

```
result loadMem(unsigned char *aMem, int aLength,
               bool aCopy, bool aTakeOwnership);
```

The aTakeOwnership parameter can be used to tell SoLoud to free the pointer once it's done with it. The aCopy parameter is here for compatibility with the other loadMem functions.

5.7.4 Openmpt.setLooping()

Adjusting the looping of a Openmpt sound does not currently have any effect. All music is set to loop by default.

5.7.5 Openmpt.setFilter()

As with any other audio source, you can attach filters to Openmpt audio sources.

```
gMusic.setFilter(0, &gLofi);
```

5.7.6 Openmpt.stop()

You can stop all instances of a Openmpt sound source with stop(). This is equivalent of calling soloud.stopAudioSource() with the sound source.

```
gMusic.stop();
```

5.7.7 Openmpt.setInaudibleBehavior()

Set the inaudible behavior of the sound. By default, if a sound is inaudible, it's paused, and will resume when it becomes audible again. With this function you can tell SoLoud to either kill the sound if it becomes inaudible, or to keep ticking the sound even if it's inaudible.

```
// Keep on talking even if I'm not around
gSpeech.setInaudibleBehavior(true, false);
```

5.7.8 Openmpt.setVolume()

Set the default volume of the instances created from this audio source.

```
gTinyVoice.setVolume(0.1);
```

5.7.9 Openmpt.setLoopPoint(), Openmpt.getLoopPoint()

If looping is enabled, the loop point is, by default, the start of the stream. The loop point can be changed, and current loop point can be queried with these functions.

```
double t = snd.getLoopPoint();
snd.setLoopPoint(t + 1); // skip 1 second more when looping
...
snd.setLoopPoint(0); // loop from start
```

Note that since looping occurs on openmpt's side, this setting currently has no effect.

5.7.10 Inherited 3d audio interfaces

Like all other audio sources, Openmpt inherits the 3d audio interfaces. Please refer to the 3d audio chapter for details on:

- Openmpt.set3dMinMaxDistance()
- Openmpt.set3dAttenuation()
- Openmpt.set3dDopplerFactor()
- Openmpt.set3dProcessing()
- Openmpt.set3dListenerRelative()
- Openmpt.set3dDistanceDelay()
- Openmpt.set3dCollider()
- Openmpt.set3dAttenuator()

5.8 SoLoud::Monotone

The SoLoud::Monotone is a replayer for MONOTONE tracker songs. MONOTONE is a pc-speaker tracker, available on GitHub at

https://github.com/MobyGamer/MONOTONE/

The SoLoud MONOTONE replayer can play MONOTONE v1 songs (only format available at the time of this writing). You can pick the number of "hardware" voices used - typically the songs are composed for a single voice (PC beeper).

The waveform used is square wave. Other waveforms can be used by modifying the soloud_monotone.cpp.

5.8.1 Monotone.clear()

You can clear all data from the Monotone object using clear:

```
void clear();
```

This is primarily used internally.

5.8.2 Monotone.load()

You tell monotone to load a file with the load function:

```
result load(const char *aFilename);
```

If loading fails, the function returns an error code.

```
SoLoud::Monotone swingin1;
swingin1.load("swingin1.mon");
```

5.8.3 Monotone.loadFile()

The loadFile() can be used to load audio from a SoLoud::File object. This is useful for integrating with virtual filesystems / packfiles, such as PhysFS.

5.8.4 Monotone.loadMem()

Alternate way of loading the file is to read from a memory buffer.

```
result loadMem(unsigned char *aMem, int aLength,
               bool aCopy, bool aTakeOwnership);
```

The aTakeOwnership parameter can be used to tell SoLoud to free the pointer once it's done with it. The aCopy parameter is here for compatibility with the other loadMem functions.

5.8.5 Monotone.setParams()

The setParams() function can be used to adjust the way SoLoud plays the MONOTONE file.

```
result setParams(int aHardwareChannels, int aWaveform);
```

Most songs are composed for a single hardware channel. SoLoud supports up to 12 hardware channels (more can be easily added by editing soloud_monotone.cpp)

For waveform, along with the default SQUARE, the SAW, SIN and SAWSIN waveforms are supported. The SAWSIN is simply saw(t)*sin(t).

5.8.6 Monotone.setLooping()

Adjusting the looping of a monotone sound does not currently have any effect. All music is set to loop by default.

5.8.7 Monotone.setFilter()

As with any other audio source, you can attach filters to monotone audio sources.

```
gMusic.setFilter(0, &gLofi);
```

5.8.8 Monotone.stop()

You can stop all instances of a monotone sound source with stop(). This is equivalent of calling soloud.stopAudioSource() with the sound source.

```
gMusic.stop();
```

5.8.9 Monotone.setInaudibleBehavior()

Set the inaudible behavior of the sound. By default, if a sound is inaudible, it's paused, and will resume when it becomes audible again. With this function you can tell SoLoud to either kill the sound if it becomes inaudible, or to keep ticking the sound even if it's inaudible.

```
// Keep on talking even if I'm not around
gSpeech.setInaudibleBehavior(true, false);
```

5.8.10 Monotone.setVolume()

Set the default volume of the instances created from this audio source.

```
gTinyVoice.setVolume(0.1);
```

5.8.11 Monotone.setLoopPoint(), Monotone.getLoopPoint()

If looping is enabled, the loop point is, by default, the start of the stream. The loop point can be changed, and current loop point can be queried with these functions.

```
double t = snd.getLoopPoint();
snd.setLoopPoint(t + 1); // skip 1 second more when looping
...
snd.setLoopPoint(0); // loop from start
```

5.8.12 Inherited 3d audio interfaces

Like all other audio sources, monotone inherits the 3d audio interfaces. Please refer to the 3d audio chapter for details on:

- Monotone.set3dMinMaxDistance()
- Monotone.set3dAttenuation()
- Monotone.set3dDopplerFactor()
- Monotone.set3dProcessing()
- Monotone.set3dListenerRelative()
- Monotone.set3dDistanceDelay()
- Monotone.set3dCollider()
- Monotone.set3dAttenuator()

5.9   SoLoud::TedSid

The SoLoud::TedSid is a replayer for TED and SID soundchip register write dumps, based on tedplay (c) 2012 Attila Grosz, used under Unlicense http://unlicense.org/.

TED is the soundchip of the commodore plus/4, and SID is the soundchip of the commodore 64.

The TED and SID songs are actually complete c64 or plus/4 programs, so in order to avoid running a complete c64 emulator in an audio engine, we only simulate the soundchips at real time. To generate the dumps, you can use the tedsid2dump.exe tool.

You can use the Soloud.getInfo() interface to query TED and SID register values while the song is playing. The SID registers are mapped to values 0-31 and the TED registers to 64-69.

5.9.1   TedSid.load()

You tell TedSid to load a file with the load function:

```
result load(const char *aFilename);
```

If loading fails, the function returns an error code.

```
SoLoud::TedSid galway;
galway.load("galway.sid.dump");
```

5.9.2   TedSid.loadMem()

Alternate way of loading the file is to read from a memory buffer.

```
result loadMem(unsigned char *aMem, int aLength,
               bool aCopy, bool aTakeOwnership);
```

SoLoud function assumes that the pointer and the data pointed will be valid as long as SoLoud needs them. You can use the aCopy parameter to tell SoLoud to take a copy of the data instead of using the pointers directly, and the aTakeOwnership parameter to tell SoLoud to free the pointer when the object is being destroyed.

5.9.3   TedSid.loadToMem()

The loadToMem() tells SoLoud to load the whole file to a memory buffer and stream it from there.

5.9.4 TedSid.loadFileToMem()

The loadFileToMem() function performs the memory loading of loadToMem() using SoLoud::File objects, same way as loadFile() does.

5.9.5 TedSid.loadFile()

The loadFile() can be used to load audio from a SoLoud::File object. This is useful for integrating with virtual filesystems / packfiles, such as PhysFS.

5.9.6 TedSid.setLooping()

Adjusting the looping of a TedSid sound does not currently have any effect. All music is set to loop by default.

5.9.7 TedSid.setFilter()

As with any other audio source, you can attach filters to monotone audio sources.

```
gMusic.setFilter(0, &gLofi);
```

5.9.8 TedSid.stop()

You can stop all instances of a monotone sound source with stop(). This is equivalent of calling soloud.stopAudioSource() with the sound source.

```
gMusic.stop();
```

5.9.9 TedSid.setInaudibleBehavior()

Set the inaudible behavior of the sound. By default, if a sound is inaudible, it's paused, and will resume when it becomes audible again. With this function you can tell SoLoud to either kill the sound if it becomes inaudible, or to keep ticking the sound even if it's inaudible.

```
// Keep on talking even if I'm not around
gSpeech.setInaudibleBehavior(true, false);
```

5.9.10 TedSid.setVolume()

Set the default volume of the instances created from this audio source.

```
gTinyVoice.setVolume(0.1);
```

5.9.11 TedSid.setLoopPoint(), TedSid.getLoopPoint()

If looping is enabled, the loop point is, by default, the start of the stream. The loop point can be changed, and current loop point can be queried with these functions.

```
double t = snd.getLoopPoint();
snd.setLoopPoint(t + 1); // skip 1 second more when looping
...
snd.setLoopPoint(0); // loop from start
```

5.9.12 tedsid2dump tool

The tedsid2dump tool can be used to dump audio chip register writes from plus/4 and c64 tunes. The tool actually runs the program code inside a limited commodore plus/4 emulator, and records the audio chip register writes as they happen, along with timestamp so they can be played back within SoLoud.

```
Usage:
tedsid2dump filename msecs [-s speed] [-m sid model] [-t tune number] [-i]

Where:
-s 1-5, song speed. 3 = single , 5 = double. Default 3
-m model 0:6581 1:8580 2:8580DB 3:6581R1. Default 1
-t the number of sub-tune to play. Default 1
-i Show information and quit
-q Quantize timestamps by 1000 ticks

Example:
tedsid2dump foobar.sid 60000 -s 5 -m 0 -t 1
```

Songs may require different replay speeds. If your song sounds wrong, you may want to try a different song speed.

If the tempo is right but some instrument sounds wrong, it's possible you're playing with a wrong SID revision. 6581 and 8580 are the most common.

It is also possible to quantize the timestamps. This may affect the way the song sounds, as the register writes won't be even close to cycle-accurate anymore, but it will also dramatically shrink the dump file sizes.

5.9.13   Dump file format

Header

Offset	Size	Information
0	5	'D' 'u' 'm' 'p' and 0 bytes signature.
5	1	SID model
6	2	2 reserved bytes (set to 0)

Timestamp

Pattern	Information
1 aaaaaaa aaaaaaaa	Timestamp. Highest bit always on, rest (a) is timestamp delta.
0 bbbbbbb cccccccc	Reg write. Highest bit always off, b is register, c is value.

Since the data is stored in x86 big-endian format, the bytes are actually swapped.

To decode, read two bytes; if the highest bit of the second byte is on, this is a timestamp, otherwise it's a register write. The timestamp delta value says how many clocks to wait until the write should be executed.

5.9.14   Inherited 3d audio interfaces

Like all other audio sources, monotone inherits the 3d audio interfaces. Please refer to the 3d audio chapter for details on:

- TedSid.set3dMinMaxDistance()
- TedSid.set3dAttenuation()
- TedSid.set3dDopplerFactor()
- TedSid.set3dProcessing()
- TedSid.set3dListenerRelative()
- TedSid.set3dDistanceDelay()
- TedSid.set3dCollider()
- TedSid.set3dAttenuator()

5.10 SoLoud::Vizsn

Vizsn is another free, but primitive speech synthesizer.

This audio source is a bit of a work in progress.

5.10.1 Vizsn.setText()

The words to be spoken are set with setText(). Calling this while the audio source is in use may cause undefined behavior.

```
// Speak the truth
gTalk.setText("You probably won't understand what I'm saying");
```

5.10.2 Vizsn.setLooping()

Adjusting the looping of a monotone sound does not currently have any effect. All music is set to loop by default.

5.10.3 Vizsn.setFilter()

As with any other audio source, you can attach filters to monotone audio sources.

```
gTalk.setFilter(0, &gLofi);
```

5.10.4 Vizsn.stop()

You can stop all instances of a monotone sound source with stop(). This is equivalent of calling soloud.stopAudioSource() with the sound source.

```
// Shut up.
gTalk.stop();
```

5.10.5 Vizsn.setInaudibleBehavior()

Set the inaudible behavior of the sound. By default, if a sound is inaudible, it's paused, and will resume when it becomes audible again. With this function you can tell SoLoud to either kill the sound if it becomes inaudible, or to keep ticking the sound even if it's inaudible.

```
// Keep on talking even if I'm not around
gTalk.setInaudibleBehavior(true, false);
```

5.10.6 Vizsn.setVolume()

Set the default volume of the instances created from this audio source.

```
gTinyVoice.setVolume(0.1);
```

5.10.7 Vizsn.setLoopPoint(), Vizsn.getLoopPoint()

If looping is enabled, the loop point is, by default, the start of the stream. The loop point can be changed, and current loop point can be queried with these functions.

```
double t = snd.getLoopPoint();
snd.setLoopPoint(t + 1); // skip 1 second more when looping
...
snd.setLoopPoint(0); // loop from start
```

5.10.8 Inherited 3d audio interfaces

Like all other audio sources, monotone inherits the 3d audio interfaces. Please refer to the 3d audio chapter for details on:

- Vizsn.set3dMinMaxDistance()
- Vizsn.set3dAttenuation()
- Vizsn.set3dDopplerFactor()
- Vizsn.set3dProcessing()
- Vizsn.set3dListenerRelative()
- Vizsn.set3dDistanceDelay()
- Vizsn.set3dCollider()
- Vizsn.set3dAttenuator()

5.11   SoLoud::Vic

The SoLoud::Vic is a vic-20 audio emulator. It is used by adjusting registers directly, like on the actual device.

This audio source is a bit of a work in progress. All instances of a single Vic object will play exactly the same audio, and registers are set at the object level.

5.11.1   Vic.setModel(), Vic.getModel()

The model of machine, between PAL and NTSC, can be set and queried. PAL is the default.

```
// Set model to NTSC
gMyVic.setModel(SoLoud::Vic::NTSC);
```

5.11.2   Vic.setRegister(), Vic.getRegister()

Registers can be set and read. All of the four registers are 8 bits wide.

```
// Increment register 2
unsigned char v = gMyVic.getRegister(2);
gMyVic.setRegister(2, v + 1);
```

5.11.3   Vic.setLooping(), Vic.setLoopPoint(), Vic.getLoopPoint()

Adjusting the looping of a vic sound does not have any effect.

5.11.4   Vic.setFilter()

As with any other audio source, you can attach filters to monotone audio sources.

```
gMusic.setFilter(0, &gLofi);
```

5.11.5   Vic.stop()

You can stop all instances of a vic sound source with stop(). This is equivalent of calling soloud.stopAudioSource() with the sound source.

```
gMusic.stop();
```

5.11.6   Vic.setInaudibleBehavior()

Set the inaudible behavior of the sound. By default, if a sound is inaudible, it's paused, and will resume when it becomes audible again. With this function you can tell SoLoud to either kill the sound if it becomes inaudible, or to keep ticking the sound even if it's inaudible.

```
// Keep on talking even if I'm not around
gSpeech.setInaudibleBehavior(true, false);
```

5.11.7   Vic.setVolume()

Set the default volume of the instances created from this audio source.

```
gTinyVoice.setVolume(0.1);
```

5.11.8   Inherited 3d audio interfaces

Like all other audio sources, monotone inherits the 3d audio interfaces. Please refer to the 3d audio chapter for details on:

- Vic.set3dMinMaxDistance()
- Vic.set3dAttenuation()
- Vic.set3dDopplerFactor()
- Vic.set3dProcessing()
- Vic.set3dListenerRelative()
- Vic.set3dDistanceDelay()
- Vic.set3dCollider()
- Vic.set3dAttenuator()

CHAPTER 6

SoLoud::Filter

Filters can be used to modify the sound some way. Typical uses for a filter are to create environmental effects, like echo, or to modify the way the speech synthesizer sounds like.

Like audio sources, filters are implemented with two classes; Filter and FilterInstance. These are, however, typically much simpler than those derived from the AudioSource and AudioInstance classes.

6.1 Filter class

```
class Example : public Filter
{
public:
  virtual FilterInstance *createInstance();
};
```

As with audio sources, the only required function is the createInstance().

6.2 FilterInstance class

```
class ExampleInstance : public FilterInstance
{
public:
    virtual void initParams(int aNumParams);

        virtual void updateParams(float aTime);

    virtual void filter(
        float *aBuffer,      int aSamples,
        int aChannels,       float aSamplerate,
        float aTime);

    virtual void filterChannel(
        float *aBuffer,      int aSamples,
        float aSamplerate,   float aTime,
        int aChannel,        int aChannels);

    virtual float getFilterParameter(
        int aAttributeId);

    virtual void setFilterParameter(
        int aAttributeId,    float aValue);

    virtual void fadeFilterParameter(
        int aAttributeId,    float aTo,
        float aTime,         float aStartTime);

    virtual void oscillateFilterParameter(
        int aAttributeId,    float aFrom,
        float aTo,           float aTime,
        float aStartTime);
};
```

The filter instance has no mandatory functions, but you may want to implement either filter()
or filterChannel() to do some actual work.

6.2.1 FilterInstance.initParams

You should call this in the constructor of your filter instance, with the number of parameters
your filter has. By convention, the first parameter should be the wet/dry parameter, where
value 1 outputs fully filtered and 0 completely original sound.

6.2.2 FilterInstance.updateParams

You should call this function in your filter or filterChannel functions to update fader values.

The mNumParams member contains the parameter count.

The mParamChanged member is bit-encoded field showing which parameters have changed. If you want to know whether parameter 3 has changed, for instance, you could do:

```
mParamChanged = 0;
updateParams(aTime);
if (mParamChanged & (1 << 3)) // param 3 changed
```

Finally, mParam array contains the parameter values, and mParamFader array contains the faders for the parameters.

6.2.3 FilterInstance.filter()

The filter() function is the main workhorse of a filter. It gets a buffer of samples, channel count, samplerate and current stream time, and is expected to overwrite the samples with filtered ones.

If channel count is not one, the layout of the buffer is such that the first channel's samples come first, followed by the second channel's samples, etc.

So if dealing with stereo samples, aBuffer first has aSamples floats for the first channel, followed by aSamples floats for the second channel.

The default implementation calls filterChannel for every channel in the buffer.

6.2.4 FilterInstance.filterChannel()

Most filters are simpler to write on a channel-by-channel basis, so that they only deal with mono samples. In this case, you may want to use the filterChannel() function instead. The default implementation of filter() calls the filterChannel() for every channel in the source.

6.2.5 FilterInstance.getFilterParameter()

This function is needed to support the changing of live filter parameters. The default implementation uses the mParam array.

Unless you do something unexpected, you shouldn't need to touch this function.

6.2.6 FilterInstance.setFilterParameter()

This function is needed to support the changing of live filter parameters. The default implementation uses the mParam array.

Unless you do something unexpected, you shouldn't need to touch this function.

6.2.7 FilterInstance.fadeFilterParameter()

This function is needed to support the changing of live filter parameters. The default implementation uses the mParamFader array.

Unless you do something unexpected, you shouldn't need to touch this function.

6.2.8 FilterInstance.oscillateFilterParameter()

This function is needed to support the changing of live filter parameters. The default implementation uses the mParamFader array.

Unless you do something unexpected, you shouldn't need to touch this function.

6.3 SoLoud::BiquadResonantFilter

The biquad resonant filter is a surprisingly cheap way to implement low and high pass filters, as well as some kind of band bass filter.

The implementation in SoLoud is based on "Using the Biquad Resonant Filter", Phil Burk, Game Programming Gems 3, p. 606.

The filter has three parameters - sample rate, cutoff frequency and resonance. These can also be adjusted on live streams, for instance to fade the low pass filter cutoff frequency for a outdoors/indoors transition effect.

The resonance parameter adjusts the sharpness (or bandwidth) of the cutoff.

```
// Set up low-pass filter
gBQRFilter.setParams(SoLoud::BiquadResonantFilter::LOWPASS, 44100, 500, 2);
// Set the filter as the second filter of the bus
gBus.setFilter(1, &gBQRFilter);
```

It's also possible to set, fade or oscillate the parameters of a "live" filter

```
gSoloud.fadeFilterParameter(
  gMusicHandle,  // Sound handle
  0,             // First filter
  SoLoud::BiquadResonantFilter::FREQUENCY,  // What to adjust
  2000,          // Target value
  3);            // Time in seconds
```

Currently, four parameters can be adjusted:

Parameter	Description
WET	Filter's wet signal; 1.0f for fully filtered, 0.0f for original, 0.5f for half and half.
SAMPLERATE	Filter's samplerate parameter
FREQUENCY	Filter's cutoff frequency
RESONANCE	Filter's resonance - higher means sharper cutoff

6.3.1 BiquadResonantFilter.setParams()

Set the parameters of the filter.

```
gBQRFilter.setParams(SoLoud::BiquadResonantFilter::LOWPASS, 44100, 500, 2);
```

Changing the parameters does not affect "live" sounds. If invalid parameters are given, the function will return error.

6.4   SoLoud::EchoFilter

The echo filter in SoLoud is a very simple one. When the sound starts to play, the echo filter allocates a buffer to contain the echo samples, and loops through this until the sound ends.

The filter does not support changing of parameters on the fly, nor does it take changing of relative play speed into account.

There are two parameters - delay and decay. Delay is the time in seconds until the echo, and decay is multiplier for the echo. If the multiplier is outside the [0..1[range, the results are unpredictable.

```
// Set up echo filter
gEchoFilter.setParams(0.5f, 0.5f);
// Set the filter as the first filter of the bus
gBus.setFilter(0, &gEchoFilter);
```

6.4.1   EchoFilter.setParams()

Set the parameters of the filter.

```
gEchoFilter.setParams(0.5f, 0.5f);
```

Changing the parameters does not affect "live" sounds. If invalid parameters are given, the function will return error.

6.5 SoLoud::LofiFilter

The lofi filter is a signal degrading filter. You can adjust both the bit depth and the sample rate of the output, and these parameters can also be adjusted (and even faded) on the fly.

```
// Set up low-pass filter
gLofiFilter.setParams(8000, 5);
// Set the filter as the first filter of the bus
gBus.setFilter(0, &gLofiFilter);
```

It's also possible to set, fade or oscillate the parameters of a "live" filter

```
gSoloud.fadeFilterParameter(
  gMusicHandle, // Sound handle
  0,            // First filter
  SoLoud::LofiFilter::BITDEPTH, // What to adjust
  2,            // Target value
  3);           // Time in seconds
```

Currently, four parameters can be adjusted:

Parameter	Description
WET	Filter's wet signal; 1.0f for fully filtered, 0.0f for original, 0.5f for half and half.
SAMPLERATE	Filter's samplerate parameter
BITDEPTH	Filter's bit-depth parameter

6.5.1 LofiFilter.setParams()

Set the parameters of the filter.

```
gLofiFilter.setParams(8000, 5);
```

Changing the parameters does not affect "live" sounds. If invalid parameters are given, the function will return error.

6.6 SoLoud::FlangerFilter

The flanger filter can be used to create a "flanger" effect on the signal. Applying this on a human voice may sound more "robotic", for instance.

```
// Set up flanger filter
gFlangerFilter.setParams(0.005f, 10);
// Set the filter as the first filter of the bus
gBus.setFilter(0, &gFlangerFilter);
```

It's also possible to set, fade or oscillate the parameters of a "live" filter

```
gSoloud.fadeFilterParameter(
    gMusicHandle,  // Sound handle
    0,             // First filter
    SoLoud::LofiFilter::WET, // What to adjust
    0,             // Target value
    3);            // Time in seconds
```

Currently, four parameters can be adjusted:

Parameter	Description
WET	Filter's wet signal; 1.0f for fully filtered, 0.0f for original, 0.5f for half and half.
FREQ	Filter's frequency
DELAY	Filter's delay

6.6.1 FlangerFilter.setParams()

Set the parameters of the filter.

```
gFlangerFilter.setParams(0.005f, 10);
```

Changing the parameters does not affect "live" sounds. If invalid parameters are given, the function will return error.

6.7 SoLoud::DCRemovalFilter

This filter tries to remove DC signal from the audio. In other words, it tries to center the waveform around 0. This can be useful if some of the input waveforms gets stuck on non-zero values for a long time.

The filter does not support changing of parameters on the fly, nor does it take changing of relative play speed into account.

The DC removal is performed by calculating the average sample value over a relatively long period of time, and subtracting this from the output.

There is one parameter - how long the averaging buffer should be. The time is in seconds.

```
// Set up DC removal filter
gDCRemovalFilter.setParams(0.1f);
// Set the filter as the first filter of the bus
gBus.setFilter(0, &gDCRemovalFilter);
```

6.7.1 DCRemovalFilter.setParams()

Set the parameters of the filter.

```
gDCRemovalFilter.setParams(0.1f);
```

Changing the parameters does not affect "live" sounds. If invalid parameters are given, the function will return error.

6.8 SoLoud::FFTFilter

The FFT filter is a short-time Fourier transform filter which can be used as basis for FFT-based effects. The base implementation does a simple tone downshifting.

The filter exists mainly to adjust the speech synthesizer's voice in strange ways. It can also be used as basis for other FFT-based filters.

6.9 SoLoud::BassboostFilter

The bassboost filter is a proof of concept FFT filter. It simply multiplies the first few bands of the FFT by the boost value.

There is one parameter - how strong the boost effect is.

```
// Set up bass boost filter
gBassboost.setParams(0.1f);
// Set the filter as the first filter of the bus
gBus.setFilter(0, &gBassboost);
```

6.9.1 BassboostFilter.setParams()

Set the parameters of the filter.

```
gBassboost.setParams(11); // ours goes to 11
```

Changing the parameters via setParams() does not affect "live" sounds. Live parameters can be set, faded or oscillated:

```
gSoloud.fadeFilterParameter(
  gMusicHandle,  // Sound handle
  0,             // First filter
  SoLoud::BassboostFilter::BOOST, // What to adjust
  0,             // Target value
  3);            // Time in seconds
```

6.10   SoLoud::WaveShaperFilter

The waveshaper filter is an experimental filter that shapes the input wave by a simple function. It is mostly meant as a voice distortion filter.

There is one parameter to adjust the severity of the effect.

```
// Set up wave shaper
gWaveshaper.setParams(0.1f, 1);
// Set the filter as the first filter of the bus
gBus.setFilter(0, &gWaveshaper);
```

6.10.1   WaveShaperFilter.setParams()

Set the parameters of the filter.

```
gWaveshaper.setParams(0.3f, 1);
```

Changing the parameters via setParams() does not affect "live" sounds. Live parameters can be set, faded or oscillated:

```
gSoloud.fadeFilterParameter(
    gMusicHandle,     // Sound handle
    0,                // First filter
    1,                // What to adjust
    0,                // Target value
    3);               // Time in seconds
```

CHAPTER 7

Other Classes

7.1 SoLoud::Bus

The mixing busses are a special case of an audio stream. They are a kind of audio stream that plays other audio streams. Mixing bus can also play other mixing busses. Like any other audio stream, mixing bus has volume, panning and filters.

Only one instance of a mixing bus can play at the same time, however; trying to play the same bus several times stops the earlier instance.

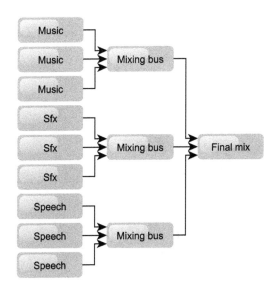

While a mixing bus doesn't generate audio by itself, playing it counts against the maximum number of concurrent streams.

Mixing busses are protected by default (i.e, won't stop playing if maximum number of concurrent streams is reached), and also marked as "must tick" (i.e, will always be present in the active voices list).

To play a stream through the mixing bus, use the bus play() command.

```
int bushandle = gSoloud.play(gBus); // Play the bus
gSoloud.setVolume(bushandle, 0.5f); // Set bus volume

int fxhandle = gBus.play(gSoundEffect); // Play sound effect through bus
gSoloud.setVolume(fxhandle, 0.5f); // set sound effect volume
```

7.1.1 Bus.setChannels()

Set the number of channels this bus should handle. Defaults to 2 (stereo).

```
gBus.setChannels(1); // set to mono
```

7.1.2 Bus.play()

Equivalent of soloud.play(), but plays the sound source through the bus instead of at "global" scope.

7.1.3 Bus.playClocked()

Equivalent of soloud.playClocked(), but plays the sound source through the bus instead of at "global" scope.

7.1.4 Bus.play3d()

Equivalent of soloud.play3d(), but plays the sound source through the bus instead of at "global" scope.

7.1.5 Bus.play3dClocked()

Equivalent of soloud.play3dClocked(), but plays the sound sounce through the bus instead of at "global" scope.

7.1.6 Bus.setVisualizationEnable()

Enable (or disable) gathering of visualization wave data from this bus.

7.1.7 Bus.calcFFT()

Calculates FFT of the sound currently playing through this bus, and returns a pointer to the result.

```
float * fft = fxbus.calcFFT();
int i;
for (i = 0; i < 256; i++)
  drawline(0, i, fft[i] * 32, i);
```

The FFT data has 256 floats, from low to high frequencies.

SoLoud performs a mono mix of the audio, passes it to FFT, and then calculates the magnitude of the complex numbers for application to use. For more advanced FFT use, SoLoud code changes are needed.

The returned pointer points at a buffer that's around as long as the bus object exists, but the data is only updated when calcFFT() is called.

For the FFT to work, you also need to enable visualization with the Bus.setVisualizationEnable() call. Otherwise the source data for the FFT calculation will not be gathered.

7.1.8 Bus.getWave()

Gets 256 samples of the sound currently playing through this bus, and returns a pointer to the result.

```
float * wav = speechbus.getWave();
int i;
for (i = 0; i < 256; i++)
  drawline(0, i, wav[i] * 32, i);
```

The returned pointer points at a buffer that's around as long as the bus object exists, but the data is only updated when getWave() is called. The data is the same that is used to generate visualization FFT data.

For this function to work properly, you also need enable visualization with the Bus.setVisualizationEnable() call. Otherwise the source data will not be gathered, and the result is undefined (probably zero).

7.1.9   Bus.getApproximateVolume()

Gets the approximate volume for output per output channel (i.e, per speaker). Returns zero for invalid parameters.

```
float ch1 = gBus.getApproximateVolume(0);
float ch2 = gBus.getApproximateVolume(1);
printf("Volume is %3.3f %3.3f", ch1, ch2);
```

Visualization needs to be enabled for this function to work.

7.1.10   Bus.setLooping(), Bus.setLoopPoint(), Bus.getLoopPoint()

Trying to change the looping state of a bus has no effect.

7.1.11   Bus.stop()

This is equivalent of calling soloud.stopAudioSource() with the sound source.

7.1.12   Bus.setFilter()

As with any other audio source, you can attach filters to busses.

```
gSfxBus.setFilter(0, &gEnvironment);
```

7.1.13   Bus.setInaudibleBehavior()

Set the inaudible behavior of the sound. By default, if a sound is inaudible, it's paused, and will resume when it becomes audible again. With this function you can tell SoLoud to either kill the sound if it becomes inaudible, or to keep ticking the sound even if it's inaudible.

```
// Kill off the sfx if they're not heard.
gSfxBus.setInaudibleBehavior(false, true);
```

7.1.14 Bus.setVolume()

Set the default volume of the bus.

```
gMusicBus.setVolume(11);
```

7.1.15 Inherited 3d audio interfaces

Like all other audio sources, the bus inherits the 3d audio interfaces. Please refer to the 3d audio chapter for details on:

- Bus.set3dMinMaxDistance()
- Bus.set3dAttenuation()
- Bus.set3dDopplerFactor()
- Bus.set3dProcessing()
- Bus.set3dListenerRelative()
- Bus.set3dDistanceDelay()
- Bus.set3dCollider()
- Bus.set3dAttenuator()

7.2 SoLoud::Queue

Queue is a special audio source which can be used to queue other audio sources. Possible uses include making endless mix of music by queueing random music patterns, streaming generated audio by cycling a few Wav objects you rewrite with loadRaw(), concatenative speech synthesis, or just simply chaining a couple sounds for some reason.

The parameters of the played audio sources are ignored. This means that all of the audio sources should have the same parameters: sample rate, channels - and that the queue must be set up to those parameters before playing.

Only one instance of a queue can play at a time.

7.2.1 Queue.play()

Queues an audio source for playback.

```
gQueue.play(gAsTimeGoesBy); // Play it, Sam
```

7.2.2 Queue.getQueueCount()

Returns the number of audio sources remaining in queue.

```
// If queue is getting short, queue another pattern.
if (gQueue.getQueueCount() < 3)
  gQueue.play(gPattern[rand()%8]);
```

7.2.3 Queue.isCurrentlyPlaying()

Check if the audio source is currently playing in queue.

```
if (gQueue.isCurrentlyPlaying(gTheGoodBit))
    print("Yay, the good bit");
```

7.2.4 Queue.setParamsFromAudioSource()

Get audio playback parameters from an audio source, instead of specifying them explicitly.

```
gQueue.setParamsFromAudioSource(gMusic);
```

7.2.5 Queue.setParams()

Set audio parameters. Use this or the setParamsFromAudioSource() before using the queue.

```
// Stereo 44.1kHz, just like the redbook ordered.
gQueue.setParams(44100, 2);
```

7.2.6 Queue.setLooping(), Queue.setLoopPoint(), Queue.getLoopPoint()

Trying to change the looping state of a queue has no effect.

7.2.7 Queue.stop()

This is equivalent of calling soloud.stopAudioSource() with the sound source.

7.2.8 Queue.setFilter()

As with any other audio source, you can attach filters to queues.

```
gMusicQueue.setFilter(0, &gConcertHall);
```

7.2.9 Queue.setInaudibleBehavior()

Set the inaudible behavior of the sound. By default, if a sound is inaudible, it's paused, and will resume when it becomes audible again. With this function you can tell SoLoud to either kill the sound if it becomes inaudible, or to keep ticking the sound even if it's inaudible.

```
// Kill off the sfx if they're not heard.
gFireworkQueue.setInaudibleBehavior(false, true);
```

7.2.10 Queue.setVolume()

Set the default volume of the queue.

```
gMusicBus.setVolume(11);
```

7.2.11 Inherited 3d audio interfaces

Like all other audio sources, the queue inherits the 3d audio interfaces. Please refer to the 3d audio chapter for details on:

- Queue.set3dMinMaxDistance()
- Queue.set3dAttenuation()
- Queue.set3dDopplerFactor()
- Queue.set3dProcessing()
- Queue.set3dListenerRelative()
- Queue.set3dDistanceDelay()
- Queue.set3dCollider()
- Queue.set3dAttenuator()

7.3 SoLoud::AudioCollider

3d sound sources may have custom audio colliders attached to them. By default, audio sources are only defined by their position and maximum range, which makes the sound sources "point sources" and omnidirectional.

With custom colliders, audio sources may be made to be bound to some area, as well as be directional.

Custom colliders are used by creating the object and passing it to an audio source via set3dCollider call:

```
MyCustomCollider cc;
gSound.set3dCollider(&cc);
gSoloud.play(gSound);
```

The set3dCollider call also takes an optional aUserData parameter. The user data as well as the collider pointer are copied to audio instances, so if you wish to launch several instances of a sound source with different collider (or just different user data), simply call the set3dCollider() before any play() calls. Disabling the collider can be done by giving the call a NULL pointer.

7.3.1 AudioCollider.collide()

To create a custom collider, extend the AudioCollider class. The class defines only one function:

```
virtual float collide(Soloud *aSoloud,
                      AudioSourceInstance *aAudioInstance,
                      int aUserData)
```

The return value is expected to be in the 0..1 range, and gives the general volume level. Soloud object and current audio instance pointers are given for convenience. Additionally, when setting the collider, the application may also set a user data integer value which is also provided to the custom collider through this call.

The custom colliders are called while processing the 3d audio in the update3dAudio() call, before any panning or attenuation is calculated. Thus, if the collide() function adjusts the audio instance's 3d position, the changes will take effect.

For example, if a "river" collider was to be created, the collider would check the player's distance to the river, and adjust the sound source's 3d position to the point closest to the player so that if the player runs along the river, the sound would be heard from the direction of the river (instead of, for instance, from just the middle of the river).

Note that calling any SoLoud functions (even to set the position of a 3d audio source) from the collide function will most likely cause the application - or at least the audio thread - to freeze due to mutex locks.

7.4 SoLoud::AudioAttenuator

3d sound sources may have custom audio attenuators attached to them. Sometimes the default options provided by SoLoud are not enough.

Custom attenuators are used by creating the object and passing it to an audio source via set3dAttenuator call:

```
MyCustomAttenuator ca;
gSound.set3dAttenuator(&ca);
gSoloud.play(gSound);
```

The attenuator pointer is copied to audio instances, so if you wish to launch several instances of a sound source with different attenuator, simply call the set3dAttenuator() before any play() calls. Disabling the attenuator can be done by giving the call a NULL pointer.

7.4.1 AudioAttenuator.attenuate()

To create a custom attenuator, extend the AudioAttenuator class. The class defines only one function:

```
virtual float attenuate(float aDistance,
                        float aMinDistance,
                        float aMaxDistance,
                        float aRolloffFactor)
```

The return value is expected to be in the 0..1 range, and gives the general volume level.

The custom attenuators are called while processing the 3d audio in the update3dAudio() call, before any panning is calculated.

Note that calling any SoLoud functions (even to set the position of a 3d audio source) from the attenuate function will most likely cause the application - or at least the audio thread - to freeze due to mutex locks.

7.5 SoLoud::File

SoLoud has a unified file i/o interface. All of the audio sources in SoLoud that require files use the File class internally and support loading through a File class.

This enables SoLoud to load from memory pointers, stream data from memory, as well as support virtual filesystems such as PhysFS by extending the File class.

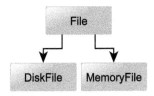

SoLoud has two File-extended classes, DiskFile which uses stdio FILE* interfaces internally, and MemoryFile which uses an in-memory buffer.

The File class only supports loading.

7.5.1 File class

The File class is abstract, and provides some helper functions.

```
class File
{
public:
    unsigned int read8();
    unsigned int read16();
    unsigned int read32();
    virtual int eof() = 0;
    virtual unsigned int read(unsigned char *aDst, unsigned int aBytes) = 0;
    virtual unsigned int length() = 0;
    virtual void seek(int aOffset) = 0;
    virtual unsigned int pos() = 0;
    virtual FILE * getFilePtr() { return 0; }
    virtual unsigned char * getMemPtr() { return 0; }
};
```

7.5.2 File.read8(), File.read16(), File.read32()

Helper functions reading 8, 16 and 32 bits from the file stream.

```
unsigned char  foo = myfile.read8();
unsigned short bar = myfile.read16();
unsigned int   baz = myfile.read32();
```

Note that the output of these helpers are unsigned, which may cause problems unless you remember to cast to signed when handling signed data, such as samples.

7.5.3 File.getFilePtr()

Returns FILE pointer if available, 0 if not. Useful to check if we're using DiskFile (or compatible), and avoids casting between File class subtypes if access to the FILE pointer is needed.

7.5.4 File.getMemPtr()

Returns memory pointer if available, 0 if not. Useful to check if we're using MemoryFile (or compatible), and avoids casting between File class subtypes if access to the memory pointer is needed.

7.5.5 File.eof()

Returns non-zero if the stream is at end of file, zero otherwise.

7.5.6 File.read()

Read up to aBytes worth of bytes from stream. Return number of bytes actually read.

7.5.7 File.length()

Return length of the file in bytes.

7.5.8 File.seek()

Seek to byte offset from beginning of stream.

7.5.9 File.pos()

Return current byte position in stream.

7.5.10 Typical File Interfaces

Using the File interface we easily support the following kind of interfaces:

```
load(const char* aFilename);
```

Load file from disk.

```
loadMem(unsigned char *aData, unsigned int aDataLength,
        bool aCopy=false, bool aTakeOwnership=true);
```

Load file from a memory pointer, optionally taking a copy of the data, and also optionally taking ownership and calling delete[] on the data when closing the file.

```
LoadFile(File *aFile);
```

Load file through File class, useful if you have custom File-extended class.

```
LoadToMem(const char *aFilename);
```

Load file from disk to a memory buffer, and then use it as a memory file.

```
LoadFileToMem(File *aFile);
```

Combination of LoadToMem and LoadFile.

Some interfaces don't supply all of the above, because they either don't need to keep the file data around, or if they are always storing the data in a memory buffer.

7.5.11 soloud_file_hack_on.h, soloud_file_hack_off.h

SoLoud comes with a pair of headers you can use to fool code which uses the FILE *interface to use File* instead.

The files use preprocessor macros to turn FILE* calls into SoLoud's wrapper function calls which in turn use the File class interfaces. Since it's a preprocessor hack, the soloud_file_hack_on.h must be included after stdio.h, or it will break stdio.h.

To switch the hack off again, you can include the soloud_file_hack_off.h, which will undefine the preprocessor macros.

Current version of the hack overrides fgetc, fread, fseek, ftell, fclose and fopen. The wrapper functions can be found in soloud_file.cpp.

7.6 Back-ends

SoLoud needs a back-end to play audio out. SoLoud ships with a bunch of back-ends with various levels of stability and latency. Creating new back-ends is relatively simple.

SoLoud speaks with the back-end with only a couple of functions, in addition to the optional mutex function pointers.

Studying the existing back-end implementations' source code, in addition to this page, will help creating new ones.

7.6.1 Soloud.postinit()

The back-end should call Soloud.postinit() once it knows what it can do.

```
void postinit(int aSamplerate, // Sample rate, in Hz
              int aBufferSize, // Buffer size, in samples
              int aFlags);     // Flags
```

The channels and flags most likely come directly from the application, while sample rate and buffer size may depend on how the back-end does things. The buffer size should be the maximum number of samples the back-end requests on one call. Making it bigger doesn't affect latency, but causes SoLoud to create larger than necessary internal mixing buffers.

7.6.2 Soloud.mix()

The back-end can call the mix function to request a number of stereo samples from SoLoud. The samples will be in float format, and the back-end is responsible for converting them to the desired output format.

```
void mix(float *aBuffer,   // Destination buffer
         int aSamples);    // Number of requested stereo samples
```

If the number of samples exceeds the buffer size set at init, the result is undefined (most likely a crash).

7.6.3 Soloud.mixSigned16()

Since so many back-ends prefer 16 bit signed data instead of float data, SoLoud also provides a mix call that outputs signed 16 bit data.

```
void mixSigned16(short *aBuffer,   // Destination buffer
                 int aSamples);    // Number of requested stereo samples
```

7.6.4 Soloud.mBackendData

This void pointer is free for the back-end to use in any way it wants. It may be a convenient place to store any buffers and other information it needs to keep around.

7.6.5 Soloud.mLockMutexFunc, Soloud.mUnlockMutexFunc

These function pointers point to functions which should lock and unlock a mutex. If they are left as NULL, they will not be called.

If they're not implemented, SoLoud will not be thread safe. This means that some shared resources, such as the channel data, may be accessed by several threads at the same time. In the worst case one thread may delete an object while another is accessing it.

7.6.6 Soloud.mMutex

Pointer to mutex data. The pointer is also passed to the lock/unlock mutex functions as a parameter.

7.6.7   Soloud.mBackendCleanupFunc

This function pointer is used by SoLoud to signal the back-end to perform cleanup; stop any threads, free any resources, etc. If NULL, not called, but may result in resource leaks and quite possibly crashes.

7.6.8   Soloud.mBackendString

Descriptive, short asciiz string about the back-end. Applications may use this to print out different audio devices for user to pick from.

7.6.9   Different back-ends

This is a non-exhaustive list of back-ends and notes regarding them.

Backend	x64	Notes
SDL/SDL2 DLL	Yes	Most tested, primary development platform. Cross-platform. Low latency.
SDL Static	?	Mostly meant for emscripten use.
SDL2 Static	Yes	Can be used to statically link to SDL2.
PortAudio	?	Cross-platform. Very low latency. Dynamic linking.
WinMM	Yes	Simplest back-end for Windows-only programs.
ALSA	Yes	Default audio interface for Linux
oss (/dev/dsp)	Yes	Simplest back-end for Linux-only programs. Experimental.
OpenAL	?	Very experimental. Very high latency; if this is your only option, you're probably better off using OpenAL directly.
WASAPI	Yes	Experimental
XAudio2	Yes	Experimental
Null driver	Yes	Can be used to use SoLoud without audio device.

Some of the backends have not been tested in x64 builds, but as long as everything is x64, there's no real reason why they don't work.

www.ingramcontent.com/pod-product-compliance
Lightning Source LLC
LaVergne TN
LVHW022319060326
832902LV00020B/3561